JAPANESE
Word-and-Phrase Book
FOR TOURISTS

JAPANESE
Word-and-Phrase Book
FOR TOURISTS

English / Français / Deutsch

Compiled by Eldora S. Thorlin, M.A.

CHARLES E. TUTTLE COMPANY
Rutland, Vermont & Tokyo, Japan

Representatives

For Continental Europe:
BOXERBOOKS, INC., *Zurich*

For the British Isles:
PRENTICE-HALL INTERNATIONAL, INC., *London*

For Australasia:
PAUL FLESCH & CO., PTY. LTD., *Melbourne*

For Canada:
HURTIG PUBLISHERS, *Edmonton*

Published by the Charles E. Tuttle Company, Inc.
of Rutland, Vermont & Tokyo, Japan
with editorial offices at
Suido 1-chome, 2-6, Bunkyo-ku, Tokyo

Copyright in Japan, 1970

by Charles E. Tuttle Co., Inc.

Library of Congress Catalog Card No. 76-113904

International Standard Book No. 0-8048-0876-7

First printing, 1970

0580-000346-4615
PRINTED IN JAPAN

TABLE OF CONTENTS

Voir la Table des Matières en français à la page 6.
Siehe Seite 7 für deutsches Inhaltsverzeichnis.

TABLE DES MATIERES

INHALTSVERZEICHNIS

INHALTSVERZEICHNIS

INTRODUCTION

Dictionaries compiled for tourists are usually of two sizes, too big and too small. Those that are comprehensive and detailed make the user spend all his time looking for the word he wants and not enjoying the sights and sounds around him. Those that are small and limited are so superficial as to be virtually useless. This book strikes a happy balance with an adequate vocabulary and a simple format.

This dictionary has a threefold value:

1. as a temporary guide to limited communication
2. as a permanent aid to basic conversation
3. as an adjunct to a formal language course

The text consists of two sections. The first is made up of English, French, and German words with their Japanese equivalents in Hepburn romanization. Many of the words are followed by an exemplifying sentence. The words and sentences are on a simple, polite conversational level and are relatively easy to pronounce.

The second section consists mainly of basic sentences essential for the tourist. Everyday situations encountered in travel, shopping, and seeing the doctor, etc., are used as topics. There are also tables for money conversion, distance, and temperature.

ENGLISH—JAPANESE

PRONOUNCING JAPANESE

The pronunciation of Japanese is relatively simple. The important things to remember are 1) that each syllable is given equal stress—*Hiroshima (Hí-ró-shi-má);* 2) that there are no silent vowels—*sake (sa-ke),* and 3) that when two or more vowels are side by side, each should be pronounced clearly—*aoi (a-o-i).*

VOWELS		CONSONANTS	
		Only the following deserve attention:	
a	father	*ch*	church
e	yes	*g*	girl
i	bean	*j*	jade
o	old	*sh*	shell
u	pool		
ā	*Hold these sounds twice as long.*		
ē (ei)	"		
ī (ii)	"		
ō	"		
ū	"		

ABBREVIATIONS:

J. = *Japanese or Japanese style*
W. = *Western or Western style*

— A —

abacus *soroban*
abscess *kanō*
absorbent cotton
  dasshimen
accident *jiko*
address *jūsho*
  Here is my a. *Kore ga
  watashi no jūsho desu.*
adhesive tape *bansōkō*
admission fee *nyūjōryō*
afternoon *gogo*
  Good a.! *Konnichi wa!*
ahead *saki*
air conditioning *reibō*
airline *kōkūro*
airline office *kōkū-
  gaisha*
airmail *kōkūbin*
  via a. *kōkūbin de*
airmail letter *kōkūbin*
airmail stamp *kōkūbin
  kitte*

airplane *hikōki*
airport *kūkō*
airsickness *hikōki-yoi*
air terminal *ēa-
  tāminaru*
à la carte *arakaruto*
alcohol *arukōru*
all right It's a.r.
  Kamaimasen.
always *itsu mo*
American (citizen)
  Amerika-jin
American Consulate
  Amerika Ryōjikan
  Where is the A. C.?
  *Amerika Ryōjikan wa
  doko desu ka?*
American Embassy
  Amerika Taishikan
  Where is the A. E.?
  *Amerika Taishikan wa
  doko desu ka?*

amusement park
  yūenchi
anaesthetic (local)
  kyokubu masui
and *to*
animal *dōbutsu*
ankle *ashikubi*
antihistamine *kō-*
  hisutamin
appendicitis *mōchōen*
apple *ringo*
appointment *yakusoku*
April *Shigatsu*
arcade (shopping) *ākēdo*
arch (at entrance to
  shrine) *torii*
arm *ude*

art gallery *garō*
artist (painter) *gaka*
ashtray *haizara*
aspirin *asupirin*
August *Hachigatsu*
aunt (your) *obasan*
aunt (my) *oba*
Australia *Ōsutoraria*
Australian (citizen)
  Ōsutoraria-jin
Australian Embassy
  Ōsutoraria Taishikan
  Where is the A. E.?
  Ōsutoraria Taishikan
  wa doko desu ka?
automobile *jidōsha*
autumn *aki*

— **B** —

baby *akambō*
baby sitter *komori*
back (of the body) *senaka*
bacon *bēkon*
bacon & eggs *bēkon to*

  tamago
bad *warui*
baggage *tenimotsu*
  excess b. *chōka-*
  tenimotsu

baggage check *tenimotsu no chikki*

balcony seat *barukonī-seki*

bamboo *take*

banana *banana*

bandage *hōtai*

bandaid *bansōkō*

bar (serving liquor) *bā*

barber *tokoya*

barbershop *tokoya*

bartender *bāten*

basement (story) *chikashitsu*

bath *furo*
　public b. (J.) *sentō*
　sauna b. *sauna-buro*
　Turkish b. *Toruko-buro*
　Where's the b.? (home) *Furo wa doko desu ka?*
　Where's the b.? (hotel) *Yokushitsu wa doko desu ka?*

bath towel *basu-taoru*

bay (of the ocean) *wan*

bean sprouts *moyashi*

beauty operator *biyōshi*

beauty shop *biyōin*

bed *betto*
　double b. *daburu betto*
　single b. *shinguru betto*

bedroom *shinshitsu*

beer *bīru*
　a bottle of b. *bīru ippon*
　a glass of b. *bīru ippai*

bellboy *beru bōi*

berth *dan-betto*
　lower b. *gedan betto*
　upper b. *jōdan betto*

bicarbonate of soda *jūsō*

bicycle *jitensha*

big *ōkii*
　too b. *ōki-sugimasu*

bill (account) *seikyūsho*

binoculars *sōgankyō*

black *kuro*

black & white film *shirokuro firumu*

black coffee *burakku-kōhī*

blanket *mōfu*

blister *mizubukure*

blood pressure *ketsuatsu*

blowfish (balloonfish, J.

15

delicacy) *fugu*
blue *burū*
bobby pin *hea-pin*
bobsled *bobbu surē*
bobsled run *bobbu surē kōsu*
boil (skin infection) *dekimono*
bookstore *hon-ya*
botanical garden *shokubutsu-en*
bottle *bin*
bottle opener *sen-nuki*
Bottoms up! *Kampai!*
box lunch (sold on RR platforms) *ekiben*
box office *kippu-uriba*
boy *otoko no ko*
brandy *burandē*
brassware *shinchū-zaiku*
bread *pan*
breakfast *chōshoku*
bridge (span) *hashi*
British (citizen) *Eikoku-jin*
British Consulate *Eikoku Ryōjikan* Where is the B. C.?

Eikoku Ryōjikan wa doko desu ka?
British Embassy *Eikoku Taishikan* Where is the B. E.? *Eikoku Taishikan wa doko desu ka?*
brocade *burokēdo*
bronchitis *kikanshi-en*
bronze *seidō*
brother (your older) *o-niisan*
brother (your younger) *otōtosan*
brother (my older) *ani*
brother (my younger) *otōto*
brown *chairo*
bruise *uchimi*
brush (hair) *hea-burashi*
bus *basu* sightseeing (tour) b. *kankō basu*
bus driver *basu no untenshu*
business card *meishi*
butter *batā*

16

— C —

cab (taxi) *takushī*
cabbage *kyabetsu*
cable(gram) *kokusai dempō*
  Where can I send a c.?
  Kokusai dempō wa doko de utemasu ka?
cake *kēki*
Call a doctor (policeman), please. *Isha (keikan) o yonde kudasai.*
Call me a taxi, please. *Takushī o yonde kudasai.*
camellia *tsubaki*
camera *kamera*
  movie c. (portable) *mūbī kamera*
camera shop *kameraya*
Canada *Kanada*
Canadian (citizen)

Kanada-jin
Canadian Embassy
  Kanada Taishikan
  Where is the C. E.?
  Kanada Taishikan wa doko desu ka?
candy *kyandē*
can opener *kan-kiri*
capsule (pill) *kapuseru*
careful
  Be c.! *Ki o tsukete!*
carp *koi*
carp streamer (Boys' Day) *koinobori*
carrot *ninjin*
cashier *suitō-gakari*
castle *shiro*
catsup *kechappu*
cauliflower *karifurawā*
celery *serorī*
cello (scotch) tape
  sero-tēpu

17

cemetery *bochi*

centimeter *senchi mētoru*

cereal
oatmeal *ōto-mīru*
corn flakes *kōnfurēkusu*

certificate of vaccination *yobō chūsha shomeisho*

chambermaid *jochū*

champagne *shampen*

change
small c. *kozeni*

cheap *yasui*

check (amount owed) *kanjō*

check-out time *chekku-auto taimu*

checkroom *kurōku*

cheese *chīzu*

cherry blossoms *sakura no hana*

chewing gum *chūin-gamu*

chicken (meat) *keiniku*

child *kodomo*

china (porcelain) *tōki*

china shop *setomonoya*

chocolate *chokorēto*

chocolate bar *chokorēto bā*

chopsticks *hashi*

chrysanthemum *kiku*

cigar *hamaki*

cigarette *tabako*
a pack of c. *tabako hitohako*

cinema (movie theater) *eigakan*

city *toshi*

clogs (J. wooden) *geta*

close
What time does it c.?
Nanji ni shimarimasu ka?

clothes (J.) *kimono*

clothes (W.) *yōfuku*

clothes hanger *hangā*

coach (RR) *kyakusha*
1st class c. *ittōsha*
2nd class c. *nitōsha*

coat *kōto*

coffee *kōhī*
a cup of c. *kōhī ippai*
black c. *burakku-kōhī*

coffee with cream

miruku iri kōhī
cold (a) *kaze*
cold (person, weather) *samui*
cold (thing) *tsumetai*
cold water *tsumetai mizu*
color film *karā firumu*
color rinse (for hair) *karā-rinsu*
comb *kushi*
conductor (train) *shashō*
Congratulations!
O-medetō gozaimasu!
constipation *bempi*
consulate *ryōjikan*
corkscrew *koruku-nuki*
corn (callus) *tako*
cough (a) *seki*

cough drop *sekidome doroppu*
cousin *itoko*
cover charge *kabā-chāji*
crab *kani*
cramp *keiren*
cream *kurīmu*
whipped c. *nama kurīmu*
credit card *kurejitto-kādo*
cross country race (ski) *dankō kyōsō*
cup *kappu*
curio (antique) *kottōhin*
curio shop *kottōhin-ya*
customs *zeikan*
customs officer *zeikanri*

— D —

daughter (your) *o-jōsan*
daughter (my) *musume*
day *hi*

It's a bad d. *Warui tenki desu.*
It's a nice d. *Iī tenki*

19

desu.

December *Jūnigatsu*

deep *fukai*

dentist *haisha*
Where can I find a d.?
Haisha wa doko desu ka?

deodorant (underarm)
asedome

department store
depāto

departure time *shuppatsu jikoku*

dessert *dezāto*

diarrhea *geri*

dining car (RR)
shokudōsha

dining room *shokudō*

dinner *yūshoku*

dish (utensil) *sara*

doctor (medical) *isha*
Call a d., please.
Isha o yonde kudasai.
Where can I find a d.?

Isha wa doko desu ka?

doll (J.) *ningyō*

double bed *daburu betto*

double room (hotel)
daburu rūmu

Down? (to elevator
operator) *Shita?*

downhill race (ski)
kakkō kyōgi

downstairs (ground
floor) *ikkai*

dress (J.) *kimono*

dress (W.) *doresu*

drinking water *nomi
mizu*

Drive slower, please.
*Motto yukkuri hashitte
kudasai.*

drugstore *kusuriya*

dry *kansō*

dry cleaning shop
kurīninguya

duty-free *menzei*

dwarf trees (J.) *bonsai*

— E —

ear *mimi*
earache *mimi no itami*
early *hayai*
earthquake *jishin*
east *higashi*
easy *yasashii*
eel *unagi*
egg *tamago*
  fried e. *medama yaki*
  hard-boiled e. *yude-tamago*
  poached e. *otoshi-tamago*
  raw e. *nama-tamago*
  scrambled e. *iri-tamago*
  soft-boiled e. *hanjuku-tamago*
eight (items) *yattsu*
eight (persons) *hachinin*
eight hundred yen *happyaku-en*
electric fan *sempūki*

electric shaver *denki kamisori*
elevator *erebētā*
embassy *taishikan*
emery board *tsume-yasuri*
Emperor (J.) *Tennō*
Empress (J.) *Kōgōheika*
enema *kanchō*
England *Igirisu*
English (language) *Eigo*
  Do you speak E.?
  Eigo o hanashimasu ka?
English (person) *Igirisu-jin*
enough
  I have enough. *Kekkō desu.*
  That's e., thank you. *Sore de kekkō desu.*
entrance *iriguchi*
envelope *fūtō*

escalator *esukarētā*

evening *yūgata*
Good e.! *Komban wa!*

excess baggage *chōka-tenimotsu*

exchange rate *kawase-sōba*
What's the e. r.?
Kawase-sōba wa ikura desu ka?

exit *deguchi*

expensive *takai*
It's too e. *Taka-sugimasu.*

express train *kyūkō*

eye *me*

eye dropper *megusuri-ire*

— F —

face *kao*

face powder *kona oshiroi*

fair (exhibition) *hakurankai*

fan (folding) *sensu*

far *tōi*

fare *ryōkin*
half f. *hangaku*

farmer *nōfu*

fat (obese) *futotta*

father (your) *o-tōsan*

father (my) *chichi*

February *Nigatsu*

fever *netsu*

fifty yen *gojū-en*

figure skater *figyā sukētā*

figure skating *figyā sukēto*

filling (tooth) *mushiba no tsumemono*

film *firumu*
black & white f. *shiro-kuro firumu*
color f. *karā-firumu*

film (motion picture)
  eiga
fine
  I'm f., thank you.
  Genki desu, arigatō.
finger *yubi*
fingernail *yubi no tsume*
fingernail polish *tsume
  no enameru*
**fingernail polish
  remover** *jokō-eki*
Fire! *Kaji!*
first-aid kit *kyūkyū-bako*
first floor (ground f.,
  American) *ikkai*
first floor (second story,
  European) *nikai*
fish *sakana*
  raw f. (J. delicacy)
  sashimi
fisherman *ryōshi*
five (items) *itsutsu*
five (persons) *gonin*
five hundred yen
  gohyaku-en
five thousand yen
  gosen-en
flash bulb *furasshu*

flight number *furaito
  nambā*
flint (for lighter) *ishi*
flower *hana*
flower arranging (J.)
  ikebana
flower shop *hanaya*
flu *infuruenza*
fog *kiri*
folk craft (J.) *mingei*
food *tabemono*
food poisoning *shoku-
  chūdoku*
foot *ashi*
foreigner *gaijin*
fork *hōku*
four (items) *yottsu*
four (persons) *yonin*
four hundred yen
  yonhyaku-en
free (of charge) *tada*
Friday *Kinyōbi*
fried egg *medama yaki*
friend *tomodachi*
frost *shimo*
frozen *reitō*
fruit *kudamono*
fruit juice *furūtsu-jūsu*

23

— G —

garden *niwa*
flower g. *hanazono*
Japanese g. *Nihon tei-en*
rock g. *sekitei*
gargle (mouth wash) *ugai*
general delivery (poste restante) *kyoku-dome*
gift *okurimono*
gin *jin*
girl *onna no ko*
glass (drinking) *koppu*
glasses (eye) *megane*
gloves *tebukuro*
gold *kin*
good *ii*
Good! (I'm happy about it.) *Yokatta desu ne!*
Good! (I understand.) *Yoroshii!*
Good afternoon!

Konnichi wa!
Goodbye! *Sayonara!*
Good evening! *Komban wa!*
Good luck! *Kōun o inoru!*
Good morning! *O-hayō gozaimasu!*
Good night! *O-yasumi nasai!*
good time
Have a g. t.! *Tanoshiku dōzo!*
I had a very g. t. *Totemo tanoshikatta.*
green *midori*
ground floor *ikkai*
guide *gaido*
tour g. *ryokō-gaido*
guidebook *annai-sho*
gums *haguki*
gynecologist *fujinka*

— H —

hair (on the head) *kami no ke*
hairbrush *hea-burashi*
haircut *sampatsu*
hairdresser *biyōshi*
hairpiece *hea-pīsu*
hairpin *hea-pin*
hair spray *hea-supurē*
half fare *hangaku*
ham *hamu*
ham & eggs *hamu-eggu*
hamburger (a) *hambāgā*
hand *te*
handbag (lady's) *hando-baggu*
handmade *tesei*
hanger (clothes) *hangā*
hangover *futsuka-yoi*
happened
 What h.? *Nani ka arimashita ka?*
happy *shiawase*

I'm h. to meet you. *Dōzo yoroshiku.*
hard-boiled egg *yude-tamago*
hat *bōshi*
hay fever *kafun netsu*
head *atama*
headwaiter *chīfu-uētā*
health certificate *kenkō shindansho*
Hello! (daytime except early morning) *Konnichi wa!*
Hello! (on the telephone) *Moshi, moshi!*
Help! *Tasukete!*
helpful
 You've been very h. *O-sewa-sama deshita.*
Help yourself, please. *Go-jiyū ni.*
here *koko ni*

25

Here's my address. *Kore ga watashi no jūsho desu.*

highball *haibōru*

hoarse *shagare-goe*

holiday *kyūjitsu*

homesickness *hōmu-shikku*

horse *uma*

hospital *byōin*

hot *atsui*

hotel (J.) *ryokan*

hotel (W.) *hoteru*

hot towel (provided in restaurants) *o-shibori*

hot water *o-yu*

hot-water bottle *yutampo*

hour (an) *ichijikan*

How? *Dono yōni?*

How are you? *Ikaga desu ka?*

How do you do? I'm happy to meet you. *Hajimemashite. Dōzo yoroshiku.*

How do you say that in Japanese? *Sore wa Nihongo de nan to iimasu ka?*

How much is it? *Ikura desu ka?*

humid *shikki ga ōi*

hundred thousand yen *jūman-en*

hundred yen *hyaku-en*

hungry I'm h. *O-naka ga suki-mashita.*

Hurry! *Hayaku!*

husband (your) *go-shujin*

husband (my) *shujin*

26

— I —

I *watashi*
I'm fine, thank you.
 Genki desu, arigatō.
I'm happy to meet
 you. *Dōzo yoroshiku.*
I'm looking for —.
 — *o sagashite imasu.*
I'm sorry! (Excuse me!)
 Gomen nasai!
I'm sorry! (I sympathize!)
 O-ki no doku desu.
ice *kōri*
ice cream *aisukurīmu*
iced tea *aisu-tī*
ice skates *aisu-sukēto*
ice skating *aisu-sukēto*
ice water *aisu-uōtā*
ill *byōki*
Immigration Office
 Nyūkoku Kanri-kyoku
immigration officer
 imin kan

incense *kō*
incense burner *kōro*
indigestion *fushōka*
infection *kansen*
information (desk)
 annaijo
injection *chūsha*
injured *kega o shita*
inn *ryokan*
insect *mushi*
insomnia *fuminshō*
interesting *omoshiroi*
 That's i. *Omoshiroi
 desu.*
international money
 order *gaikoku yūbin-
 gawase*
interpreter *tsūyaku*
iodine *yōdochinki*
iris (flower) *ayame*
iron (for pressing) *airon*
island *shima*

27

itinerary *ryotei*	**ivory** *zōge*

— J —

jade *hisui*	**Japan National Railways (JNR)** *Kokutetsu*
jam (preserves) *jamu*	**Japan Travel Bureau (JTB)** *Nihon Kōtsū Kōsha*
January *Ichigatsu*	
Japan *Nippon*	
Japan Air Lines (JAL) *Nihon Kōkū*	**jelly** *zerī*
Japanese (citizen) *Nihon-jin*	**jet plane** *jettoki*
Japanese (made in Japan) *Nihon sei*	**jewelry shop** *hōseki-ten*
	juice *jūsu*
	July *Shichigatsu*
Japanese (language) *Nihongo*	**June** *Rokugatsu*

— K —

ketchup *kechappu*	**kilometer** *kiro(mētoru)*
key *kagi*	**kleenex** (J.) *chirigami*
kilo(gram) *kiro(guramu)*	**kleenex** (W.) *kurīnek-*

kusu
knee *hiza*
know
　Do you k.? *Shitte*

imasu ka?
I don't k. *Shirimasen.*
I know. *Shitte imasu.*

— L —

lacquer ware *shikki*
ladies' room *o-tearai*
　Where's the l. r.?
　*O-tearai wa doko desu
　ka?*
lake *mizu-umi*
landing (airplane)
　chakuriku
lantern (J. metal) *tōrō*
lantern (J. paper)
　chōchin
lantern (J. stone)
　ishi-dōrō
large *ōkii*
laryngitis *kōtōen*
late *osoi*
laxative *gezai*
leather *kawa*

left (opposite of right)
　hidari
　Turn l., please. *Hidari
　e magatte kudasai.*
leg *ashi*
lemon *remon*
lemonade *remonēdo*
letter (epistle) *tegami*
lettuce *retasu*
lighter
　cigarette l. *raitā*
lighter fluid *raitā-eki*
light meter *roshutsu-kei*
like
　Do you like it? *Suki
　desu ka?*
　I don't like it. *Kirai
　desu.*

29

liniment

I like it. *Suki desu.*
liniment *nuri-gusuri*
lipstick *kuchibeni*
liquor store *sakaya*
liter *rittoru*
little *chiisai*
local anaesthetic
   kyokubu masui
local train *futsū ressha*
long (in length) *nagai*
long (in time) *nagai aida*
Look! *Minasai!*
looking for
   I'm looking for —.
   — *o sagashite imasu.*

Look out! *Abunai!*
lost
   I'm lost. *Michi ni*
   mayoimashita.
lost property office
   ishitsu-butsu atsukaijo
lotion
   hand l. *hando-rōshon*
   eye l. *megusuri*
lower berth (train)
   gedan betto
lump (swelling) *kobu*
lunch *chūshoku*
   box l. (sold on RR
   platforms) *ekiben*

— M —

magazine *zasshi*
man *otoko no hito*
manager *shihainin*
Manhattan (cocktail)
   Manhattan
manicure *manikyua*
manicurist *manikyua-*

shi
many *takusan*
map *chizu*
March *Sangatsu*
martini *mātīnī*
massage *massāji*
   scalp m. *atama no*

massāji

masseur *otoko-amma*

masseuse *onna-amma*

match (for lighting)
matchi

matter
What's the m.?
Dō shimashita ka?

May *Gogatsu*

maybe *tabun*

May I see that?
Sore o misete kudasai.

mayonnaise *mayonēzu*

meal (breakfast, lunch,
etc.) *shokuji*

medicine *kusuri*

medicine dropper
tenteki

meet
I'm happy to m. you.
Dōzo yoroshiku.

melon *meron*

men's room *tearai*
Where's the m. r.?
*Tearai wa doko desu
ka?*

menu *menyū*

meter *mētoru*

midnight *mayonaka*

milk *miruku*
a glass of m.
miruku ippai

million yen *hyakuman-
en*

mineral oil *mineraru
oiru*

mineral water *tansansui*

minute (in time) *fun*

mirror *kagami*

Miss *-san*

mistake *machigai*

molar *kyūshi*

Monday *Getsuyōbi*

money *o-kane*

month *tsuki*

monument *kinenhi*

moon *tsuki*

more (additional) *motto*

morning *asa*
Good m.! *O-hayō
gozaimasu!*

mother (your) *o-kāsan*

mother (my) *haha*

motorcycle *ōtobai*

mountain *yama*

mouth *kuchi*

31

movie camera (portable) *mūbī-kamera*
movies *eiga*
movie theater *eigakan*
Mr. *-san*

Mrs. *-san*
much *takusan*
museum *hakubutsukan*
music *ongaku*
mustard *karashi*

— N —

nail file (metal) *tsume-yasuri*
nail polish *tsume no ena-meru*
nail-polish remover *jokō-eki*
name *namae*
napkin *nafukin*
narrow *semai*
national park *kokuritsu-kōen*
nausea *hakike*
near *chikai*
negative (photo) *nega*
nervous *shinkeishitsu*
new *atarashii*
news (TV, radio) *nyūzu*

newspaper *shimbun*
New Zealand *Nyū Jīrando*
New Zealand Embassy *Nyū Jīrando Taishikan*
Where is the N. Z. E.? *Nyū Jīrando Taishikan wa doko desu ka?*
New Zealander *Nyū Jīrando-jin*
nice *ii*
night *yoru*
Good n.! *O-yasumi nasai!*
night club *naito-kurabu*
nine (items) *kokonotsu*
nine (persons) *kunin*

nine hundred yen *kyū-hyaku-en*
No! (Don't do that!) *Dame!*
No. (I don't like it.) *Kirai desu.*
No. (That's wrong.) *Chigaimasu.*
noisy *yakamashii*
No more, thank you *Kekkō desu.*
noodles (J.) *udon, soba*
noon *hiru*
north *kita*
nose *hana*

nosebleed *hanaji*
nose drops *hanagusuri*
nothing *nanimo*
November *Jūichigatsu*
novocaine *nobokain*
now *ima*
number *bangō*
    flight n. *furaito nambā*
    room n. *heya-bangō*
    seat n. *zaseki-bangō*
    telephone n. *denwa-b.*
    track no. *-bansen*
nurse *kangofu*
nylons (stockings) *sutokkingu*

— O —

ocean *taiyō*
o'clock *-ji*
October *Jūgatsu*
oil painting *abura-e*
ointment *nuri-gusuri*
O.K.! *Okē!*
old (person) *toshiyori*

old (thing) *furui*
omelet *omuretsu*
once *ichido*
one (item) *hitotsu*
one (person) *hitori*
one-way ticket *katamichi kippu*

onion *tamanegi*

open
  What time does it o.?
  Nanji ni akimasu ka?

opener
  bottle o. *sen-nuki*
  can o. *kan-kiri*

operation (surgical)
  shujutsu

operator (telephone)
  kōkanshu

orange (fruit) *orenji*
  tangerine *mikan*

orange juice *orenji-jūsu*

orchestra seat *ōkesutora bokkusu*

Oriental (person)
  Tōyōjin

overseas call (telephone) *kokusai denwa*

oyster *kaki*

— P —

Pacific Ocean *Taiheiyō*

pack of cards *torampu hitokumi*

pack of cigarettes
  tabako hitohako

pagoda *tō*

pain *itami*

painter (artist) *gaka*

palace *kyūden*

paper *kami*
  Japanese p. (hand-

made) *washi*
  newspaper *shimbun*
  toilet p. *toiretto-pēpā*
  writing p. *binsen*

parasol *higasa*

Pardon me! *Gomen nasai!*

park *kōen*

passport *pasupōto*

pastry *okashi*

peach *momo*

peanut *pīnatsu*

pear (J.) *nashi*

pearl *shinju*

pearl necklace *shinju no nekkuresu*

peas *mame*

pen (ball-point) *bōru pen*

pencil *empitsu*

penicillin *penishirin*

pepper (ground black) *koshō*

pepper shaker *koshō-ire*

persimmon *kaki*

perspiration *ase*

pharmacy *kusuriya*

phonograph record *rekōdo*

photo *shashin*

photo supply shop *kameraya*

pickles (J.) *tsukemono*

picture postcard *ehagaki*

pill *gan-yaku*

pillow *makura*

pilot (airplane) *pairotto*

pin
safety p. *anzen-pin*

straight p. *machi-bari*

pipe (for smoking) *paipu*

pipe tobacco *paipu tabako*

plate (dish) *sara*

platform
RR station p. *puratto hōmu*

platform ticket (RR) *nyūjōken*

play (theatrical) *shibai*

Please. (Take it. Go ahead.) *Dōzo.*

Please. (Bring me. Give me.) *Kudasai.*

Please. (Help me. Wait on me.) *O-negai shimasu.*

poached egg *otoshi-tamago*

pocket *poketto*

policeman *keikan*
Call a p., please. *Keikan o yonde kudasai.*

police station *keisatsusho*

polish remover (nail polish) *jokō-eki*

35

pool (for swimming)
  pūru
porcelain *jiki*
pork *butaniku*
pork cutlet *pōku*
  katsuretsu
porter *akabō*
postage stamp *kitte*
postbox *posuto*
post office *yūbinkyoku*
potato *jagaimo*
  sweet p. (J.) *satsuma-*
  imo
pottery *setomono*
present (gift) *okurimono*
pretty *kirei*
price *nedan*

price of admission
  nyūjōryō
print (J.) *hanga*
print (photo) *purinto*
projector (movie)
  eishaki
projector (slide) *gentōki*
prune juice *puramu-*
  jūsu
prunes (stewed)
  nikomi-puramu
psychiatrist *seishinka-i*
public bath (J.) *sentō*
public toilet *kōshū benjo*
pudding *purin*
purple *murasaki*

— Q —

quickly *hayaku* | **quiet** *shizuka*

— R —

racetrack (horse)
  keibajō
radio *rajio*
  transistor r. *toranjisutā
  rajio*
radish (J.) *daikon*
railroad car *kyakusha*
railroad station *eki*
railroad track *senro*
rain *ame*
raincoat *rēnkōto*
rainstorm *bōfū-u*
rainy season *tsuyu*
rash (skin eruption)
  jimmashin
rattan *tō*
raw egg *nama-tamago*
raw fish (J. delicacy)
  sashimi
raw silk (material)
  rō shiruku
razor blade *kamisori no*

ha
ready
  Are you r.?
  Jumbi wa ii desu ka?
  I'm not r. *Mada desu.*
  I'm r. *Jumbi ga deki-
  mashita.*
  When will it be r.?
  Itsu dekimasu ka?
receipt *uketori*
red *aka*
registered letter
  kakitome
Repeat that, please.
  Mō ichido itte kudasai.
reservation *yoyaku*
  I have a r. *Watashi wa
  yoyaku o shite imasu.*
reserved seat *shitei-seki*
reserved table *yoyaku-
  seki*
resort *hoyō*

ski r. *sukī-jō*
summer r. *hishochi*
restaurant (J.) *ryōriya*
restaurant (W.)
resutoran
revue (dance) *rebyū*
rice (cooked) *gohan*
rice (uncooked) *kome*
rice cracker (J.) *sembei*
rice paddy *tambo*
right (opposite of left)
migi
Turn r., please.
Migi e magatte kudasai.
right
That's r. *Sō desu.*

rinse (color, for hair)
karā rinsu
river *kawa*
road *dōro*
rock garden *sekitei*
roll (bread) *rōru-pan*
roller (hair) *amikarā*
room (house or hotel)
heya
room & board *geshuku*
room number *heya-
bangō*
rose (flower) *bara*
round *marui*
round-trip ticket
ōfuku kippu

— S —

saccharin *sakkarin*
sad *kanashii*
safety belt *anzen beruto*
safety pin *anzen-pin*
salad *sarada*
salesclerk *ten-in*

salmon *sake*
salt *shio*
salt shaker *shio-ire*
salt water *shio-mizu*
same (the) *onaji*
sand *suna*

ship

sandwich *sandoitchi*
sash (J.) *obi*
Saturday *Doyōbi*
saucer (for cup) *kozara*
sausage *sōsēji*
Say! *Ano ne!*
scalp massage *atama no massāji*
scissors *hasami*
Scotch (whisky) *Sukotchi*
scotch (cello) tape *serotēpu*
scrambled egg *iritamago*
screen (J. folding) *byōbu*
screen (J. translucent sliding door) *shōji*
scroll (J. hanging) *kakemono*
sea *umi*
seafood *gyokairui*
seat (theater, train, etc.) *seki*
seat number *zasekibangō*
sea urchin (edible) *uni*

seaweed (dried, edible) *nori*
second (in time) *byō*
second floor (American) *nikai*
second floor (European) *sankai*
sedative *chinseizai*
Separate checks, please. *Betsubetsu ni kanjō o shite kudasai.*
September *Kugatsu*
seven (items) *nanatsu*
seven (persons) *shichinin*
seven hundred yen *nanahyaku-en*
shampoo-set *shampūsetto*
sharp *surudoi*
shaver (electric) *denki kamisori*
shaving brush *higesori burashi*
shaving cream *shēbingu kurīmu*
sheet *shītsu*
sherbet *shābetto*
ship (a) *fune*

39

shoe *kutsu*

shoeshine *kutsu migaki*

shop (a) *mise*

shopping *kaimono*

short (length) *mijikai*

short (opposite of tall)
hikui

shot (injection) *chūsha*

shower bath *shawā*

shrimp *ebi*

shrine (Shinto) *jinja*

sick
I feel s. *Kibun ga
waruku narimashita.*

sightseeing bus *kankō
basu*

silk (material) *kinu*
raw s. *rō shiruku*

silver *gin*

single bed *shinguru
betto*

single room (hotel)
shinguru rūmu

sister (your older)
o-nēsan

sister (your younger)
imōtosan

sister (my older) *ane*

sister (my younger)
imōto

six (items) *muttsu*

six (persons) *rokunin*

six hundred yen
roppyaku-en

size (clothing) *saizu*

skater *sukētā*

skates
ice s. *aisu sukēto*

skating *sukēto*

skating rink *sukēto-jō*

ski *sukī*

ski binding *sukī
baindingu*

ski boots *sukī-gutsu*

skier *sukīyā*

skiing *sukī*

ski jump *sukī jampu*

ski lift *sukī rifuto*

skin (human) *hifu*

skin (animal or fruit)
kawa

ski poles *sukī sutokku*

ski resort *sukī-jō*

sky *sora*

skyscraper *matenrō*

slalom *kaiten*

sled *sori*

sleeping car (RR) *shindaisha*

sleeping pill *suimin-yaku*

slide (photo) *suraido*

slower
Drive s., please. *Motto yukkuri hashitte kudasai.*

slowly *yukkuri*
Speak more s., please. *Motto yukkuri hanashite kudasai.*

small *chiisai*

small change *kozeni*

snack *sunakku*

snow *yuki*

snowstorm *fubuki*

soap *sekken*

soft-boiled egg *hanjuku-tamago*

son (your) *musuko-san*

son (my) *musuko*

song *uta*

soon *mamonaku*

sore throat *nodo no itami*

sorry
I'm s. (Excuse me.) *Gomen nasai.*
I'm s. (I sympathize.) *O-ki no doku desu.*

soup (J.)
clear s. *suimono*
bean paste s. *miso shiru*

soup (W.) *sūpu*

soup bowl *sūpu-zara*

soup spoon *sūpu-supūn*

south *minami*

souvenir *miyage*

soy sauce *shōyu*

speak
Do you s. English? *Eigo o hanashimasu ka?*
Speak more slowly, please. *Motto yukkuri hanashite kudasai.*

spoon *supūn*
soup s. *sūpu-supūn*
table s. *ōsaji*
tea s. *chasaji*

sport *supōtsu*

sprain (a) *nenza*

spring (season) *haru*

square (shape) *shikaku*

squid *ika*
stairway *kaidan*
stamp
  airmail s. *kōkūbin kitte*
  postage s. *kitte*
star *hoshi*
station (RR) *eki*
statue *zō*
steak *sutēki*
stewardess (airplane)
  suchūwādesu
stomach ache *i no itami*
stone lantern *ishi-dōrō*
Stop here! *Koko de ii desu!*
straight ahead *massugu*
  Go s. a. *Massugu itte kudasai.*
straight pin *machi-bari*
strawberries *ichigo*
straw mat (J.) *tatami*
street *tōri*
Street *-dōri*
streetcar *densha*
string beans *saya-ingen*
student *seito*

sty (eye infection)
  monomorai
subway *chikatetsu*
subway station
  chikatetsu no eki
sugar *satō*
suit (man's) *sebiro*
suitcase *toranku*
summer *natsu*
sun *taiyō*
Sunday *Nichiyōbi*
sunglasses *sangurasu*
sunshine *nikkō*
suntan *hiyake*
suntan oil *hiyake-oiru*
supper *yūshoku*
sure
  Are you s.? *Tashika desu ka?*
surgeon *geka-i*
surgery (operation)
  shujutsu
sweet potato (J.)
  satsuma-imo
syringe (for enema)
  kanchōki

— T —

tablespoon *ōsaji*
takeoff (airplane) *ririku*
tall *takai*
tangerine *mikan*
tape
  adhesive t. *bansōkō*
  scotch (cello) t. *sero-tēpu*
tape recorder *tēpu-rekōdā*
tax-exempt *menzei*
taxi *takushū*
  Call me a t., please.
  Takushū o yonde kudasai.
taxi driver *takushū no untenshu*
tea (J. green) *o-cha*
tea (W. black) *kōcha*
  iced t. *aisu-tī*
tea ceremony (J.) *chanoyu*
teacher *sensei*

teacup (J.) *chawan*
teacup (W.) *kōcha-jawan*
teaspoon *chasaji*
telegram *dempō*
  Where can I send a t.?
  Dempō wa doko de utemasu ka?
telegraph office *denshin-kyoku*
telephone *denwa*
  Where is a t.?
  Denwa wa doko desu ka?
telephone number *denwa-bangō*
telephone operator *kōkanshu*
television *terebi*
temple (Buddhist) *tera*
ten (items) *tō*
ten (persons) *jūnin*
ten thousand yen

43

ichiman-en

ten yen *jū-en*

Thanks! *Arigatō!*

Thank you. (in general)
Arigatō gozaimasu.

thatched roof *kayabuki-yane*

That's enough, thank you. *Sore de kekkō desu, arigatō.*

That's interesting. *Omoshiroi desu.*

That's right. *Sō desu.*

That's wrong. *Sore wa chigaimasu.*

that one *sore*

theater (for plays) *gekijō*

there *asoko*

Thief! *Dorobō!*

think

I don't t. so.
Sō omoimasen.

I t. so. *Sō omoimasu.*

thirsty

I'm t. *Nodo ga kawaki-mashita.*

this one *kore*

thousand yen *sen-en*

three (items) *mittsu*

three (persons) *sannin*

three hundred yen
sambyaku-en

Thursday *Mokuyōbi*

ticket (train & plane)
kippu

one-way t. *katamichi kippu*

platform t. (RR)
nyūjōken

round-trip t. *ōfuku kippu*

ticket window *mado-guchi*

time

What t. is it?
Nanji desu ka?

tired

I'm t. *Tsukaremashita.*

toast *tōsuto*

tobacco *tabako*

tobacco pouch
tabako-ire

today *kyō*

toe *ashi no yubi*

toenail *ashi no tsume*

toilet *tearai*

public t. *kōshū benjo*
toilet paper (J.)
chirigami
toilet paper (W.)
toiretto-pēpā
tomato *tomato*
tomato juice *tomato-jūsu*
tomorrow *ashita*
tonight *komban*
tonsillitis *hentōsen-en*
tooth *ha*
toothache *ha no itami*
toothbrush *ha-burashi*
toothpaste *ha-migaki*
toothpick *tsumayōji*
tour *ryokō*
tour bus *kankō basu*
tour guide *ryokō-gaido*
tourist *kankōkyaku*
towel *taoru*
bath t. *basu-taoru*
hot t. (provided in restaurants) *o-shibori*
town *machi*
toy *omocha*
track
race t. (horse) *keibajō*

RR t. *senro*
track number
-bansen
traffic light *kōtsū-shingō*
train
express t. *kyūkō*
local t. *futsū-ressha*
train conductor *shashō*
tranquilizer (pill)
chinseizai
transistor radio
toranjisutā rajio
travel agency *kōtsū-kōsha*
traveler's check
toraberā-chekku
tree *ki*
trip (journey) *ryokō*
Tuesday *Kayōbi*
tuna fish *maguro*
tunnel *tonneru*
Turn left, please.
Hidari e magatte kudasai.
Turn right, please.
Migi e magatte kudasai.

45

TV channel

TV channel *terebi channeru*
twin beds *tsuin-betto*
two (items) *futatsu*

two (persons) *futari*
two hundred yen *nihyaku-en*
typhoon *taifū*

— U —

ugly *minikui*
umbrella (J. oiled paper) *bangasa*
umbrella (W.) *ama-gasa*
uncle (your) *ojisan*
uncle (my) *oji*
understand
  Do you u.?
  Wakarimasu ka?
  I don't u.

  Wakarimasen.
  I u. *Wakarimashita.*
United States of America *Amerika Gasshūkoku*
Up? (to elevator operator) *Ue?*
upper berth *jōdan betto*
upstairs *nikai*
usherette (theater) *annai-nin*

— V —

vacant
  Is this seat v.?
  Kono seki wa aite

  imasu ka?
vaccination (smallpox) *shutō*

46

vaccination certificate *yobō chūsha shōmeisho*	**village** *mura*
valley *tani*	**visa** *biza*
vegetables *yasai*	**vitamin pills** *bitamin-jōzai*
very *taihen*	
Very good! *Taihen ii!*	**vodka** *uokka*
view *keshiki*	**volcano** *kazan*

— W —

Wait a minute!
Chotto matte!
waiter *kyūji*
head w. *chīfu-uētā*
Waiter!
Chotto o-negai shimasu!
waiting room
machiai-shitsu
waitress *uētoresu*
Waitress!
Chotto o-negai shimasu!
wallet *saifu*
want

What do you w.?
Nan deshō ka?
want to buy—I w. t.
b. a Japanese doll.
Nihon ningyō o kaitai.
want to go—I w. t. g.
to the Ginza.
Ginza e ikitai.
want to ride—I w. t.
r. on the monorail
Monorēru ni noritai.
want to visit—I w. t.
v. Kyoto. *Kyōto e ikitai.*
warm *atatakai*

47

washcloth *tenugui*

water *mizu*

  a glass of w. *mizu ippai*

  cold w. *tsumetai mizu*

  drinking w. *nomi mizu*

  hot w. *o-yu*

  ice w. *aisu-uōtā*

  salt w. *shio-mizu*

watercolor (painting) *suisaiga*

waterfall *taki*

watermelon *suika*

way

  Can you show me the way?

  Annai shite kuremasu ka?

  I've lost my way.

  Michi ni mayoimashita.

  Which way is it? (direction)

  Dochira no hōkō desu ka?

W. C. *toire*

weather *tenki*

Wednesday *Suiyōbi*

welcome

  You're w.

  Dō-itashimashite.

west *nishi*

wet *nureta*

What? *Nani?*

What do you want?

  Nan deshō ka?

What happened?

  Nani ka arimashita ka?

What's the exchange rate? *Kawase-sōba wa ikura desu ka?*

What's the matter?

  Dō shimashita ka?

What's this (that)?

  Kore (sore) wa nan desu ka?

What time is it?

  Nanji desu ka?

When? *Itsu?*

Where? *Doko?*

Where can I find a doctor (dentist)?

  Isha (haisha) wa doko desu ka?

Where can I send a cable (telegram)?

  Kokusai dempō (dempō) wa doko de utemasu ka?

Where is a telephone?
Denwa wa doko desu ka?

**Where's the ladies'
room?** *O-tearai wa
doko desu ka?*

**Where's the men's
room?** *Tearai wa doko
desu ka?*

Which one? (of two)
Dochira?

Which one? (of more
than two) *Dore?*

whipped cream
nama kurīmu

whiskey (whisky)
uisukī
double w. *daburu
uisukī*

white *shiro*

Who? *Donata?*

Who's there?
Donata desu ka?

Why? *Dō shite?*

wide *hiroi*

wife (your) *okusan*

wife (my) *tsuma*

wig *katsura*

wind (the) *kaze*

wine *budōshu*

wine list *wain-risuto*

winter *fuyu*

woman *onna no hito*

woodblock print (J.)
hanga

woods *mori*

wristwatch *ude-dokei*

Write it down, please.
Sore o kaite kudasai.

writing paper *binsen*

wrong
That's w.
Sore wa chigaimasu.

wrong number
(telephone) *bangō-
chigai*

— **X** —

x-ray *rentogen*

— **Y** —

year *toshi*
yellow *kiiro*
Yes. *Hai.*
yesterday *kinō*

you *anata*
young *wakai*
youth hostel
   yūsu-hosuteru

— **Z** —

zipper *jippā*

zoo *dōbutsu-en*

FRANÇAIS—JAPONAIS

PRONONCIATION DE JAPONAIS

La prononciation du japonais est relativement simple. Les choses les plus importantes à rappeler, ce sont que 1) chaque syllabe est donnée la même force—*Hiroshima (Hí-ró-shí-má)*; 2) il n'y a pas de voyelles muettes—*sake (sa-ke)*; 3) quand deux voyelles différentes se trouvent ensemble, chacune conserve son propre son —*aoi (a-o-i)*.

VOYELLES		CONSONNES	
		Il ne faut faire attention ici qu'aux suivantes:	
a	bal	*ch*	tchèque
e	belle	*g*	garçon
i	visite	*j*	jazz
o	tomate	*sh*	cheval
u	mouche		
ā	Celles-ci sont caractérisées par une prolongation de son.		
ē (ei)	,,		
ī (ii)	,,	**ABREVIATIONS:**	
ō	,,	j. = *japonais ou style japonais*	
ū	,,	e. = *européen ou style européen*	

— A —

abaque (boulier compteur) *soroban*

abcès *kanō*

accident *jiko*

addition (restaurant, bar) *kanjō*

Additions individuelles, s.v.p. *Betsubetsu ni kanjō o shite kudasai.*

adresse *jūsho*
Voici mon a. *Kore ga watashi no jūsho desu.*

aéroport *kūkō*

aéroport terminal *ēa-tāminaru*

agent (de police) *keikan*
Faites venir un a., s.v.p. *Keikan o yonde kudasai.*

aigu *surudoi*

aimer

Je l'aime. *Suki desu.*

Je ne l'aime pas. *Kirai desu.*

L'aimez-vous? *Suki desu ka?*

à la carte *arakaruto*

alcool *arukōru*

algue sèche (mangeable) *nori*

aller
Ça va bien. *Kamaimasen.*
Comment allez-vous? *Ikaga desu ka?*
Je vais bien, merci. *Genki desu, arigatō.*

Allô! (au téléphone) *Moshi, moshi!*

allumette *matchi*

ambassade *taishikan*

Ambassade Canadienne *Kanada Taishikan*

53

Où se trouve l'Ambassade Canadienne?
Kanada Taishikan wa doko desu ka?

Ambassade Française
Furansu Taishikan
Où se trouve l'Ambassade Française?
Furansu Taishikan wa doko desu ka?

ami *tomodachi*

ampoule (cloque)
mizubukure

ampoule flash *furasshu*

amuser
Amusez-vous bien!
Tanoshiku dōzo!
Je me suis bien amusé.
Totemo tanoshikatta.

amygdalite *hentōsen-en*

anesthésie locale
kyokubu masui

anglais
Parlez-vous a.?
Eigo o hanashimasu ka?

anguille *unagi*

animal *dōbutsu*

année *toshi*

antihistamine
kō-hisutamin

antiquité *kottōhin*

août *Hachigatsu*

appareil (photographique) *kamera*

appendicite *mōchōen*

après-midi *gogo*
Bon a.-m.!
Konnichi wa!

aquarelle (peinture)
suisaiga

arbre *ki*

arbres (plantes) nains
(j.) *bonsai*

arcade (des magasins)
ākēdo

arc d'entrée (temple
Shinto) *torii*

argent *o-kane*

argent (métal) *gin*

**arrangement de
fleurs** (j.) *ikebana*

Arrêtez ici, s.v.p.
Koko de ii desu.

ascenseur *erebētā*

aspirine *asupirin*

assez

C'est a., merci.
*Sore de kekkō desu,
arigatō.*
J'en ai a. *Kekkō desu.*
assiette *sara*
assiette creuse
sūpu-zara
**Attendez un instant,
s.v.p.**
Chotto matte kudasai.
Attention! *Abunai!*
atterrissage *chakuriku*
auberge (j.) *ryokan*
Auberge de jeunesse
yūsu-hosuteru
Au feu! *Kaji!*

aujourdhui *kyō*
Au revoir! *Sayonara!*
Au secours! *Tasukete!*
autobus *basu*
autocar touristique
kankō basu
automne *aki*
automobile *jidōsha*
avant
en avant *saki*
avion *hikōki*
avion à réaction *jettoki*
A votre santé!
Kampai!
avril *Shigatsu*

— B —

baby sitter (gardienne
d'enfants) *komori*
bacon *bēkon*
bagages *tenimotsu*
excès de b.
chōka-tenimotsu

baguettes en bois (avec
lesquelles on mange
du vivre japonais)
hashi
baie (de la mer) *wan*
bain *furo*

bain public (j.) *sentō*
bain Turc *Toruko-buro*
bambou *take*
banane *banana*
banderole de carpes
  (j.) *koinobori*
bar (boîte de nuit) *bā*
barbier *tokoya*
barman *bāten*
bas
  en b. *ikkai*
  En bas? (au liftier)
  Shita?
bas nylon *sutokkingu*
bâtons de ski
  surī sutokku
beaucoup *takusan*
bébé *akambō*
beurre *batā*
bicarbonate de soude
  jūsō
bicyclette *jitensha*
bientôt *mamonaku*
bière *bīru*
  une bouteille de b.
  bīru ippon
bifteck *sutēki*
bijouterie *hōseki-ten*

billet (avion, train)
  kippu
billet d'aller
  katamichi kippu
billet d'aller et retour
  ōfuku kippu
billet de quai *nyūjōken*
biscuit (j., fait à la
  farine de riz) *sembei*
blague à tabac
  tabako-ire
blaireau
  higesori burashi
blanc *shiro*
blessé *kega o shita*
bleu *burū*
bleu (meurtrissure)
  uchimi
bob *bobbu surē*
bois *mori*
boîte (de nuit)
  naito-kurabu
boite à lettres
  posuto
bon *ii*
Bon! (Je comprends.)
  Yoroshii!
Bon après-midi!

Konnichi wa!

bonbons *kyandē*

Bonjour! (le matin, de
bonne heure)
O-hayō gozaimasu!

Bonjour! (le midi,
l'après-midi)
Konnichi wa!

bon marché *yasui*

Bonne Chance!
Kōun o inoru!

Bonsoir! *Komban wa!*

Bonsoir! (tard)
O-yasumi nasai!

bouche *kuchi*

bouillotte *yutampo*

bouteille *bin*

bracelet-montre
ude-dokei

briquet (cigarettes)
raitā

brocart *burokēdo*

bronchite *kikanshi-en*

bronze *seidō*

brosse à cheveux

hea-burashi

brosse à dents
ha-burashi

brouillard *kiri*

brun *chairo*

bruyant *yakamashii*

**Bureau d'Immigra-
tion** *Nyūkoku Kanri-
kyoku*

**bureau de la ligne
aérienne** *kōkū-gaisha*

bureau de location
kippu-uriba

bureau de poste
yūbinkyoku

**bureau des objets
perdus et trouvés**
ishitsu-butsu atsukaijo

bureau de touristes
kōtsū-kōsha

**Bureau Japonais de
Tourisme (JTB)**
Nihon Kōtsū Kōsha

bureau télégraphique
denshin-kyoku

57

— C —

câblogramme
  kokusai dempō
  Où puis-je envoyer un
  c.? *Kokusai dempō wa*
  doko de utemasu ka?
cacaouètes *pīnatsu*
cadeau *okurimono*
café *kōhī*
  une tasse de c.
  kōhī ippai
café au lait
  miruku iri kōhī
café noir *burakku-kōhī*
caissier *suitō-gakari*
calmar *ika*
calment *chinseizai*
camélia *tsubaki*
caméra (film, portatif)
  mūbī kamera
Canada *Kanada*
Canadien *Kanada-jin*
capsule (pilule)

  kapuseru
carotte *ninjin*
carpe *koi*
carré *shikaku*
carte (du jour) *menyū*
carte (plan) *chizu*
carte de crédit
  kurejitto-kādo
carte des vins
  wain-risuto
carte de visite *meishi*
carte postale *ehagaki*
cascade *taki*
casse-croûte *sunakku*
cave (étage) *chikashitsu*
ceinture (j.) *obi*
ceinture de protection
  anzen beruto
céleri *serorī*
celui-ci *kore*
celui-là *sore*
cendrier *haizara*

centimetre
senchi mētoru

cent mille yen
jūman-en

cent yen *hyaku-en*

cérémonie de thé (j.)
chanoyu

cerisier *sakura no hana*

certificat de santé
kenkō shindansho

**certificat de vaccina-
tion** *yobō chūsha shō-
meisho*

chaîne (télévision)
channeru

chaleureux *atatakai*

chambre (hôtel,
maison) *heya*

chambre à coucher
shinshitsu

**chambre à deux per-
sonnes** (hôtel)
daburu rūmu

**chambre à une per-
sonne** (hôtel)
shinguru rūmu

champagne *shampen*

champ de courses

keibajō

chanson *uta*

chapeau *bōshi*

château *shiro*

chaud *atsui*

chauffeur de taxi
takushi no untenshu

chaussures *kutsu*

chaussures de ski
sukī-gutsu

chemin *dōro*

**Chemin de Fer Na-
tional de Japon
(JNR)** *Kokutetsu*

chèque de voyage
toraberā-chekku

cher (coûteux) *takai*
C'est trop c.
Taka-sugimasu.

chercher
Je cherche —.
— *o sagashite imasu.*

cheval *uma*

cheveux *kami no ke*

cheville *ashikubi*

chewing-gum
chūin-gamu

chirurgien *geka-i*

chocolat *chokorēto*
chou *kyabetsu*
chou-fleur *karifurawā*
chrysanthème *kiku*
ciel *sora*
cigare *hamaki*
cigarette *tabako*
   un paquet de c.
   tabako hitohako
cimetière *bochi*
cinéma (théâtre)
   eigakan
cinéma *eiga*
cinq (choses) *itsutsu*
cinq (personnes) *gonin*
cinq cents yen
   gohyaku-en
cinq mille yen
   gosen-en
cinquante yen *gojū-en*
cireur de chaussures
   kutsu migaki
ciseaux *hasami*
citron *remon*
citron pressé *remonēdo*
clef *kagi*
cliché (photo) *nega*
climatisation *reibō*

coiffeuse *biyōshi*
collier de perles
   shinju no nekkuresu
Combien coût'-il?
   Ikura desu ka?
Comment? (De quelle
   manière?) *Dono yōni?*
Comment allez-vous?
   Ikaga desu ka?
commissariat de
   police *keisatsusho*
complet *sebiro*
comprendre
   Comprenez-vous?
   Wakarimasu ka?
   Je comprends.
   Wakarimashita.
   Je ne comprends pas.
   Wakarimasen.
compte-gouttes *tenteki*
conducteur (autobus)
   basu no untenshu
Conduisez plus lente-
   ment, s.v.p. *Motto*
   yukkuri hashitte
   kudasai.
Conduisez tout droit,
   s.v.p.

Massugu itte kudasai.

confiture *jamu*

connaissance
Enchanté de faire
votre c. *Hajimemashite.*
Dōzo yoroshiku.

constipation *bempi*

consulat *ryōjikan*

Consulat Canadien
Kanada Ryōjikan
Où se trouve le C. C.?
*Kanada Ryōjikan wa
doko desu ka?*

Consulat Français
Furansu Taishikan
Où se trouve le C. F.?
*Furansu Taishikan wa
doko desu ka?*

contrôleur (train)
shashō

cor (orteil) *tako*

cornichons (j.)
tsukemono

côtelette de porc
pōku katsuretsu

couchette inférieure
(train) *jōdan betto*

couchette supérieure

(train) *gedan betto*

**coup de téléphone
d'outre-mer**
kokusai denwa

coupe de cheveux
sampatsu

cours du change
kawase-sōba
Quel est le c. d. c.?
*Kawase-sōba wa ikura
desu ka?*

course de bob
bobbu surē kōsu

court (longueur) *mijikai*

court (hauteur) *hikui*

cousin *itoko*

couverture de laine
mōfu

crabe *kani*

crampe *keiren*

crayon *empitsu*

crème *kurīmu*

crème fouettée
nama kurīmu

crevette *ebi*

cross à skis
dankō kyōsō

cuillère *supūn*

cuillère à bouche *ōsaji*
cuillère à café *chasaji*
cuillère à soupe
  sūpu-supūn

cuivre jaune
  shinchū-zaiku
cure-dents *tsumayōji*

— D —

D'accord! *Okē!*
de bonne heure *hayai*
decembre *Jūnigatsu*
décollage (avion)
  ririku
déjeuner *chūshoku*
déjeuner en boîte (j.,
  vendu aux quais du
  chemin de fer) *ekiben*
demain *ashita*
demi-place *hangaku*
dent *ha*
dentiste *haisha*
  Où puis-je trouver un
  d.? *Haisha wa doko
  desu ka?*
Dépêchez-vous!
  Hayaku!
descente à skis

  kakkō kyōgi
désodorisant (sous-
  bras) *asedome*
désolé
  Je suis d.
  O-ki no doku desu.
dessert *dezāto*
deux (choses) *futatsu*
deux (personnes) *futari*
deux cents yen
  nihyaku-en
diarrhée *geri*
dimanche *Nichiyōbi*
dîner *yūshoku*
direction
  J'ai perdu la d.
  Michi ni mayoimashita.
  Pourriez-vous m'in-
  diquer la d.?

Annai shite kuremasu ka?

Quelle est la d.?

Dochira no hōkō desu ka?

disque *rekōdo*

dissolvant (vernis à ongles) *jokō-eki*

dix (choses) *tō*

dix (personnes) *jūnin*

dix mille yen *ichiman-en*

dix yen *jū-en*

doigt *yubi*

ongle de d.

yubi no tsume

dos *senaka*

douane *zeikan*

douanier *zeikanri*

douche *shawā*

drap *shitsu*

droit

tout d. *massugu*

droite *migi*

Tournez à d., s.v.p.

Migi e magatte kudasai.

— E —

eau *mizu*

un verre d'e.

mizu ippai

eau chaude *o-yu*

eau de mer *shio-mizu*

eau-de-vie *burandē*

eau froide *tsumetai mizu*

eau glacée *aisu-uōtā*

eau minérale *tansansui*

eau potable *nomi mizu*

Ecoutez! *Ano ne!*

écran (j., pliant) *byōbu*

écrire

Voulez-vous l'é., s.v.p.

Sore o kaite kudasai.

empereur (j.) *Tennō*

emplettes *kaimono*

encens *kō*
encensoir *kōro*
encore *motto*
enfant *kodomo*
enflure *kobu*
enroué *shagare-goe*
entrée *iriguchi*
entremets *purin*
enveloppe *fūtō*
épingle *machi-bari*
épingle à cheveux
  hea-pin
épingle de sûreté
  anzen-pin
épreuve (photo) *purīnto*
éruption (de la peau)
  jimmashin
escalier *kaidan*
escalier roulant
  esukarētā

essence à briquet
  raitā-eki
est *higashi*
estampe (j.) *hanga*
et *to*
été *natsu*
étoile *hoshi*
étranger *gaijin*
étroit *semai*
étudiant *seito*
éventail (pliant) *sensu*
excès de bagages
  chōka-tenimotsu
Excusez-moi!
  Gomen nasai!
exempt de droits
  menzei
exposition *hakurankai*
express (train) *kyūkō*

— F —

facile *yasashii*
facture (de vente)
  seikyūsho

faim
  J'ai f.
  O-naka ga sukimashita.

64

français

faire

Il fait beau.

Ii tenki desu.

Il fait mauvais.

Warui tenki desu.

Faites venir un méde-cin (agent) s.v.p.

Isha (keikan) o yonde kudasai.

Faites venir un taxi, s.v.p. *Takushī o yonde kudasai.*

fatigué

Je suis f.

Tsukaremashita.

faute *machigai*

fauteuil d'orchestre *ōkesutora bokkusu*

faux numéro (au télé-phone) *bangō-chigai*

Félicitations!

O-medetō gozaimasu!

femme (une) *onna no hito*

femme (votre) *okusan*

femme (ma) *tsuma*

femme de chambre *jochū*

fer à repasser *airon*

fermer

A quelle heure ferme-t-il? *Nanji ni shimari-masu ka?*

fermeture de ski *sukī baindingu*

fermeture éclair *jippā*

fermier *nōfu*

feu

Au f.! *Kaji!*

feu de circulation *kōtsū-shingō*

février *Nigatsu*

fièvre *netsu*

figure (visage) *kao*

fille (votre) *o-jōsan*

fille (ma) *musume*

fils (votre) *musuko-san*

fils (mon) *musuko*

fleur *hana*

fleuriste *hanaya*

fois (une) *ichido*

foulure *nenza*

fourchette *hōku*

fraises *ichigo*

Français *Furansu-jin*

français (langue)

65

Furansugo
France *Furansu*
frère (votre plus âgé)
o-niisan
frère (votre plus jeune)
otōtosan
frère (mon plus âgé) *ani*
frère (mon plus jeune)
otōto

froid (choses) *tsumetai*
froid (personnes, temps)
samui
fromage *chīzu*
fruit *kudamono*
fruits de la mer
gyokairui
furoncle *dekimono*

— **G** —

galerie (d'art) *garō*
gants *tebukuro*
garçon *otoko no ko*
garçon (serviteur) *kyūji*
Garçon! *Chotto o-negai
shimasu!*
gare *eki*
gargarisme *ugai*
gâteau *kēki*
gauche *hidari*
Tournez à g., s.v.p.
*Hidari e magatte
kudasai.*

gelé *reitō*
gelée *zerī*
gencives *haguki*
genou *hiza*
gentil *ii*
gérant *shihainin*
gin *jin*
givre *shimo*
glace (eau glacée) *kōri*
glace (crème glacée)
aisukurīmu
gouttes pour le nez
hanagusuri

gouttes pour les yeux
   megusuri
grand (taille) *ōkii*
grand (hauteur) *takai*
grand magasin *depāto*
gratte-ciel *matenrō*
gratuit *tada*
grippe *infuruenza*
groom (hôtel) *beru bōi*

gros (obèse) *futotta*
gueule de bois
   futsuka-yoi
güichet *mado-guchi*
guide (brochure)
   annai-sho
guide de voyage
   ryokō-gaido
gynécologue *fujinka*

— H —

hamburger (un)
   hambāgā
haricots verts *saya-
   ingen*
haut
   en h. *nikai*
   En h.? (au liftier) *Ue?*
heure (une) *ichijikan*
heure (l') *-ji*
   Quelle h. est-il?
   Nanji desu ka?
heure de départ
   shuppatsu-jikoku

**heure de donner
   congé** (hôtel)
   chekku-auto taimu
heureux *shiawase*
hier *kino*
hiver *fuyu*
homme *otoko no hito*
hôpital *byōin*
hôtel (j.) *ryokan*
hôtel (e.) *hoteru*
hôtesse (de l'air)
   suchūwādesu
huile minérale

mineraru oiru	**huit cents yen**
huit (choses) *yattsu*	*happyaku-en*
huit (personnes)	**huitre** *kaki*
hachinin	**humide** *shikki ga ōi*

— **I** —

ici *koko ni*	**infirmière** *kangofu*
Il n'y a pas de quoi.	**insecte** *mushi*
Dō-itashimashite.	**insomnie** *fuminshō*
immigration	**intéressant** *omoshiroi*
Bureau d'I.	C'est i.
Nyūkoku Kanri-kyoku	*Omoshiroi desu.*
officier d'i. *imin kan*	**interprète** *tsūyaku*
île *shima*	**intoxication alimen-**
impératrice (j.)	**taire** *shokuchūdoku*
Kōgōheika	**iode** *yōdochinki*
imperméable *rēnkōto*	**iris** (fleur) *ayame*
indigestion *fushōka*	**itinéraire** *ryotei*
infection *kansen*	**ivoire** *zōge*

— J —

jade *hisui*
jambe *ashi*
jambon *hamu*
janvier *Ichigatsu*
Japon *Nippon*
Japonais (citoyen)
　Nihon-jin
japonais (fabriqué au
　Japon) *Nihon sei*
japonais (langue)
　Nihongo
　Comment dites-vous
　cela en j.? *Sore wa
　Nihongo de nan to
　iimasu ka?*
japonerie *kottōhin*
jardin *niwa*
jardin botanique
　shokubutsu-en
jardin de fleurs
　hanazono
jardin de rocaille (j.)

　sekitei
jardin japonais
　Nihon tei-en
jaune *kiiro*
je *watashi*
jeu de cartes
　torampu hito kumi
jeudi *Mokuyōbi*
jeune *wakai*
jeune fille *onna no ko*
joli *kirei*
jouet *omocha*
jour *hi*
jour de fête *kyūjitsu*
journal *shimbun*
juillet *Shichigatsu*
juin *Rokugatsu*
jumelles *sōgankyō*
jus *jūsu*
jus de fruit *furūtsu-jūsu*
jus de prune *puramu-
　jūsu*

jus de tomate
tomato-jūsu

jus d'orange *orenji-jūsu*

— K —

kilo(gramme)
kiro(guramu)
kilomètre

kiro(mētoru)
kleenex (j.) *chirigami*
kleenex (e.) *kurīnekkusu*

— L —

là-bas *asoko*
lac *mizu-umi*
lacque (article japonais)
shikki
lacque (pour les
cheveux) *hea-supurē*
laid *minikui*
lait *miruku*
un verre de l.
miruku ippai
laitue *retasu*

lame de rasoir
kamisori no ha
lampe flash *furasshu*
lanterne (j., en métal)
tōrō
lanterne (j., en papier)
chōchin
lanterne (j., en pierre)
ishi-dōrō
large *hiroi*
laryngite *kōtōen*

lavement (clystère)
kanchō
lavette *tenugui*
laxatif *gezai*
légumes *yasai*
lentement *yukkuri*
Conduisez plus l., s.v.p.
*Motto yukkuri
hashitte kudasai.*
Parlez plus l., s.v.p.
*Motto yukkuri
hanashite kudasai.*
Lequel? (des deux)
Dochira?
Lequel? (de plus de
deux) *Dore?*
lettre (épître) *tegami*
lettre aérienne *kōkūbin*
lettre recommandée
kakitome
librairie *hon-ya*
ligne aérienne *kōkūro*
**Ligne Aérienne
Japonaise (JAL)**
Nihon Kōkū
lime à ongles (en métal)

tsume-yasuri
lime émeri
tsume-yasuri
liniment *nuri-gusuri*
lit *betto*
lit à deux personnes
daburu betto
lit à une personne
shinguru betto
litre *rittoru*
lits jumeaux *tsuin-
betto*
loin *tōi*
long (longeur) *nagai*
long (temps) *nagai aida*
lotion (pour les mains)
hando-rōshon
lotion pour bronzer
hiyake-oiru
lumière de soleil
nikkō
lundi *Getsuyōbi*
lune *tsuki*
lunettes *megane*
lunettes de soleil
sangurasu

71

— M —

M. -san

magasin mise

magasin à photo
  kameraya

magasin d'antiquités
  kottōhin-ya

magasin de porce-
  laine setomonoya

magazine zasshi

magnétophone
  tēpu-rekōdā

mai Gogatsu

main te
  fait à la m. tesei

maintenant ima

maître d'hôtel
  chīfu-uētā

malade byōki
  Je me sens m.
  Byōki desu.

mal à la gorge
  nodo no itami

mal à l'estomac
  i no itami

mal à l'oreille
  mimi no itami

mal aux dents
  ha no itami

mal de l'air hikōki-yoi

mal du pays
  hōmushikku

mandarine mikan

mandat international
  gaikoku yūbin-gawase

manteau kōto

manucure manikyua

manucure (personne)
  manikyua-shi

marchand de vin
  sakaya

mardi Kayōbi

mari (votre) go-shujin

mari (mon) shujin

mars Sangatsu

martini *mātīnī*

massage *massāji*

massage de scalpe
atama no massāji

masseur *otoko-amma*

masseuse *onna-amma*

matin *asa*

mauvais *warui*

mayonnaise *mayonēzu*

médecin *isha*
Faites venir un m.,
s.v.p. *Isha o yonde
kudasai.*
Où puis-je trouver un
m.? *Isha wa doko
desu ka?*

médicament *kusuri*

melon *meron*

même chose *onaji*

mer *umi*

Merci! *Arigatō!*

Merci. (J'en ai assez.)
Kekkō desu.

Merci beaucoup. (en
général) *Arigatō go-
zaimasu.*

mercredi *Suiyōbi*

mère (votre) *o-kāsan*

mère (ma) *haha*

mètre *mētoru*

métro *chikatetsu*

mets *tabemono*

midi *hiru*

mille yen *sen-en*

million de yen
hyakuman-en

minuit *mayonaka*

minute *fun*

miroir *kagami*

Mlle *-san*

Mme *-san*

mois *tsuki*

molaire *kyūshi*

monnaie *kozeni*

montagne *yama*

monument *kinenhi*

motocyclette *ōtobai*

mouillé *nureta*

moutarde *karashi*

musée *hakubutsukan*

musique *ongaku*

— N —

natte de paille (j.)
  tatami
nausée *hakike*
neige *yuki*
nerveux *shinkeishitsu*
neuf (choses) *kokonotsu*
neuf (personnes) *kunin*
neuf cents yen
  kyuhyaku-en
nez *hana*
noir *kuro*
nom *namae*
Non! (Ne faites pas
  cela!) *Dame!*
Non. (Je ne l'aime pas.)
  Kirai desu.
Non. (Vous avez tort.)
  Chigaimasu.
non
  Je crois que n.
  Sō omoimasen.

nord *kita*
note (hôtel) *kanjō*
nouilles (j.) *udon, soba*
nourriture *tabemono*
nouveau *atarashii*
nouvelles *nyūzu*
novembre *Jūichigatsu*
novocaïne *nobokain*
nuit *yoru*
numéro *bangō*
numéro de chambre
  heya-bangō
numéro de siège
  zaseki-bangō
numéro de téléphone
  denwa-bangō
  faux n. *bangō chigai*
numéro de voie
  -bansen
numéro de vol
  furaito nambā

— O —

océan *taiyō*
Océan Pacifique
 Taiheiyō
octobre *Jūgatsu*
oeil *me*
oeuf *tamago*
oeuf à la coque
 hanjuku-tamago
oeuf brouillé *iri-tamago*
oeuf cru *nama-tamago*
oeuf dur *yude-tamago*
oeuf poché
 otoshi-tamago
oeufs au bacon
 bēkon to tamago
oeufs au jambon
 hamu-eggu
oeuf sur le plat
 medama-yaki
officier d'immigra-
 tion *imin kan*
oignon *tamanegi*

omelette *omuretsu*
omnibus *futsū ressha*
oncle (votre) *ojisan*
oncle (mon) *oji*
ongle de doigt
 yubi no tsume
ongle d'orteil
 ashi no tsume
opération (chirurgicale)
 shujutsu
or *kin*
orange (fruit) *orenji*
 manderine *mikan*
oreille *mimi*
oreiller *makura*
orgelet *monomorai*
Oriental *Tōyōjin*
orteil *ashi no yubi*
 ongle d'o.
 ashi no tsume
Où ? *Doko?*
ouate *dasshimen*

ouest *nishi*
Oui. *Hai.*
oui
  Je crois que o.
  Sō omoimasu.
Où puis-je envoyer un câblogramme (télégramme)?
  Kokusai dempō (dempō) wa doko de utemasu ka?
Où puis-je trouver un médecin (dentiste)?
  Isha (haisha) wa doko desu ka?
Où se trouvent les toilettes? (femmes)
  O-tearai wa doko desu ka?
Où se trouvent les toilettes? (hommes)
  Tearai wa doko desu ka?
Où se trouve le téléphone? *Denwa wa doko desu ka?*
ouvre-boîte *kan-kiri*
ouvre-bouteille *sen-nuki*
ouvreuse (théâtre) *annai-nin*
ouvrir
  A quelle heure ouvre-t-il?
  Nanji ni akimasu ka?

— P —

pain *pan*
pain grillé *tōsuto*
palais *kyūden*
pansement *hōtai*
pansement individuel *bansōkō*
papier *kami*
papier à écrire *binsen*

papier collant *sero-tēpu*

papier fait à la main (j.)
washi

papier hygiénique (j.)
chirigami

papier hygiénique (e.)
toiretto-pēpā

paquet de cigarettes
tabako hitohako

parapluie (j., en papier)
bangasa

parapluie (e.) *ama-gasa*

parasol (j.) *higasa*

parc *kōen*

parc national
kokuritsu-kōen

Pardonnez-moi!
Gomen nasai!

Parlez plus lentement,
s.v.p. *Motto yukkuri
hanashite kudasai.*

Parlez-vous anglais?
Eigo o hanashimasu ka?

passeport *pasupōto*

pastèque *suika*

pastille (pour une toux)
sekidome doroppu

pâte dentifrice

---

ha-migaki

patinage à glace
aisu sukēto

patinage de fantaisie
figyā sukēto

patineur *sukētā*

patineur de fantaisie
figyā sukētā

patinoire *sukēto-jō*

patins à glace
aisu sukēto

patisserie *okashi*

peau (d'une personne)
hifu

peau (d'un animal ou
de fruit) *kawa*

pêche *momo*

pêcheur *ryōshi*

peigne *kushi*

peine (douleur) *itami*

peintre *gaka*

peinture à l'huile
abura-e

pellicule (à photo)
firumu

pellicule en blanc et
noir *shirokuro firumu*

pellicule en couleur

karā-firumu
penicilline *penishirin*
pension (chambre et
aliment) *geshuku*
perdre
Je me suis perdu.
Michi ni mayoimashita.
père (votre) *o-tōsan*
père (mon) *chichi*
perle *shinju*
perruque *katsura*
petit *chiisai*
petit déjeuner
chōshoku
petit pain *rōru-pan*
peut-être *tabun*
pharmacie *kusuriya*
photo *shashin*
pièce (au théâtre)
shibai
pied *ashi*
pierre à briquet *ishi*
pilote *pairotto*
pilule *gan-yaku*
pince (pour les cheveux)
hea-pin
pipe *paipu*
piqûre *chūsha*

piscine *pūru*
place (théâtre, train,
etc.) *seki*
Est-ce que cette p. est
libre? *Kono seki wa
aite imasu ka?*
place réservée
shitei-seki
plaire
S'il vous plaît.
(Prennez-le. Conti-
nuez.) *Dōzo.*
S'il vous plaît. (Appor-
tez-le-moi. Donnez-
le-moi.) *Kudasai.*
S'il vous plaît.
(Aidez-moi. Servez-
moi.) *O-negai shimasu.*
plombage (dent)
mushiba no tsumemono
pluie *ame*
poche *poketto*
poire (j.) *nashi*
pois (petits) *mame*
poisson *sakana*
poisson cru (j., mangeable) *sashimi*
poisson gonflé

(délicatesse j.) *fugu*
poivre *koshō*
poivrière *koshō-ire*
pommade *nuri-gusuri*
pomme *ringo*
pomme de terre
  jagaimo
  patate (j.) *satsuma-imo*
pont *hashi*
porc *butaniku*
porcelaine *tōki*
porcelaine de Chine
  tōki
portefeuille *saifu*
porte glissante (j.)
  shōji
porte-manteau *hangā*
porteur *akabō*
posemètre *roshutsu-kei*
poste aérienne *kōkūbin*
  par avion *kōkūbin de*
poste restante
  kyoku-dome
postiche *hea-pīsu*
poterie *yakimono*
poudre (de riz)

  kona oshiroi
poulet (chair) *keiniku*
poupée (j.) *ningyō*
Pourquoi? *Dō shite?*
pousses d'haricots
  moyashi
premier étage *nikai*
Prenez garde!
  Ki o tsukete!
printemps *haru*
prix *nedan*
prix (frais de voyage)
  ryōkin
prix d'entrée (couvert)
  kabā-chāji
proche *chikai*
professeur *sensei*
profond *fukai*
projecteur (films)
  eishaki
projecteur (diapositifs)
  gentōki
projection (vue) *suraido*
pruneau (cuit)
  nikomi-puramu
psychiatre *seishinka-i*

— Q —

quai (chemin de fer)
  puratto hōmu
Quand? *Itsu?*
quatre (choses) *yottsu*
quatre (personnes)
  yonin
quatre cents yen
  yonhyaku-en
quelque chose *naki ka*
quelque fois *toki-doki*
Qu'est-ce que c'est

que ceci (cela)? *Kore*
  (sore) wa nan desu ka?
Qu'est-ce qu'il y a?
  Nani ka arimashita ka?
Qui? *Donata?*
Qui est là?
  Donata desu ka?
Quoi? *Nani?*
quoi
  Il n'y a pas de q.
  Dō-itashimashite.

— R —

radiographie *rentogen*
radis (j.) *daikon*
raison
  Vous avez r. *Sō desu.*
rasoir électrique

  denki kamisori
reçu (de vente) *uketori*
Regardez! *Minasai!*
rendez-vous *yakusoku*
renseignements *annai*

repas *shokuji*
Répétez, s.v.p. *Mō ichido itte kudasai.*
réservation *yoyaku*
  J'ai une r. *Watashi wa yoyaku o shite imasu.*
restaurant (j.) *ryōriya*
restaurant (e.) *resutoran*
revue (au théâtre) *rebyū*
rez-de-chaussée *ikkai*
rhume *kaze*
rhume des foins *kafun netsu*
rien *nanimo*
rinçage de couleur (pour les cheveux)

karā rinsu
rivière *kawa*
riz (cuit) *gohan*
riz (cru) *kome*
rizière *tambo*
robe (j.) *kimono*
robe (e.) *doresu*
rond *marui*
rose (fleur) *bara*
rotin *tō*
rouge *aka*
rouge à lèvres *kuchibeni*
rouleaux (pour les cheveux) *amikarā*
Rue *-dōri, tōri*

— S —

sable *suna*
sac à main *hando-baggu*
saccharine *sakkarin*
saignement du nez *hanaji*
salade *sarada*

salière *shio-ire*
salle à manger *shokudō*
salle d'attente *machiai-shitsu*
salle de bain *furoba*

Où se trouve la s.d.b.?
(maison) *Furoba wa
doko desu ka?*
Où se trouve la s.d.b.?
(hôtel) *Yokushitsu wa
doko desu ka?*
salon de beauté *biyōin*
samedi
Doyōbi
sandales en bois (j.)
geta
sandwich *sandoitchi*
sans droits *menzei*
sauce de soya *shōyu*
sauce tomate *kechappu*
saucisse *sōsēji*
saumon *sake*
saut à ski *sukī jampu*
savoir
Je ne sais pas.
Shirimasen.
savon *sekken*
savon à barbe
shēbingu kurīmu
scotch (whisky)
Sukotchi
sec *kansō*
seconde (instant) *byō*

secours
Au s.! *Tasukete!*
sel *shio*
sept (choses) *nanatsu*
sept (personnes)
shichinin
sept cents yen
nanahayku-en
septembre *Kugatsu*
seringue *kanchōki*
serveuse *uētoresu*
Serveuse!
Chotto o-negai shimasu!
Servez-vous, s.v.p.
Go-jiyū ni.
serviette *nafukin*
serviette (essuie-mains)
taoru
serviette de bain *basu-
taoru*
serviette mouillée
(servie avant de man-
ger aux restaurants
japonais) *o-shibori*
servir
Vous m'avez bien
servi. *O-sewa-sama
deshita.*

**shampooing et mise
en plis** *shampū-setto*
siège au balcon
  barukonī-seki
six (choses) *muttsu*
six (personnes) *rokunin*
six cents yen
  roppyaku-en
ski *sukī*
skieur *sukīyā*
slalom *kaiten*
soeur (votre plus âgée)
  o-nēsan
soeur (votre plus jeune)
  imōto-san
soeur (ma plus âgée) *ane*
soeur (ma plus jeune)
  imōto
soie (tissu) *kinu*
soie grège (tissu)
  rō shiruku
soif
  J'ai s. *Nodo ga
  kawakimashita.*
soir *yūgata*
  Bonsoir! *Komban wa!*
  ce s. *komban*
soleil *taiyō*

lumière de soleil *nikkō*
somnifère *suimin-yaku*
sortie *deguchi*
soucoupe *kozara*
soupe (j., bouillon)
  suimono
(j., pâte d'haricots)
  misoshiru
soupe (e.) *sūpu*
souper *yūshoku*
souvenir (cadeau)
  miyage
sparadrap *bansōkō*
sport *supōtsu*
station (climatérique)
  hoyō
station balnéaire
  hishochi
station de métro
  chikatetsu no eki
station de ski *sukī-jō*
statue *zō*
stylo à bille *bōru pen*
sucre *satō*
sud *minami*
sûr
  Etes-vous s.?
  Tashika desu ka?

— T —

tabac *tabako*

tabac pour le pipe
paipu-tabako

tableau pendant (j.)
kakemono

table reservée
yoyaku-seki

tablette de chocolat
chokorēto

taille (vêtements) *saizu*

tante (votre) *obasan*

tante (ma) *oba*

tard *osoi*

tarif (d'entrée) *nyūjōryō*

tasse *kappu*

tasse à thé (j.) *chawan*

tasse à thé (e.)
kōcha-jawan

taxi *takushī*
Faites venir un t., s.v.p.
*Takushī o yonde
kudasai.*

teint bronzé *hiyake*

teinturier *kurīninguya*

télégramme *dempō*
Où puis-je envoyer un
t.? *Dempō wa doko de
utemasu ka?*

téléphone *denwa*
Où se trouve le t.?
*Denwa wa doko desu
ka?*

téléphoniste *kōkanshu*

télésiège *sukī rifuto*

télévision *terebi*

tempête de neige
fubuki

tempête de pluie
bōfū-u

temple (bouddhiste)
tera

temple (shintoiste)
jinja

temps (état de l'at-

84

mosphère) *tenki*
temps pluvieux
(saison) *tsuyu*
tension artérielle
ketsuatsu
tête *atama*
thé (j., vert) *o-cha*
thé (e., noir) *kōcha*
théâtre *gekijō*
thé glacé *aisu-tī*
thon *maguro*
ticket de consigne
tenimotsu no chikki
timbre aérien
kōkūbin kitte
timbre postal *kitte*
tire-bouchon *koruku-*
nuki
toilettes (femmes)
o-tearai
Où se trouvent les t.?
O-tearai wa doko desu
ka?
toilettes (hommes)
tearai
Où se trouvent les t.?
Tearai wa doko desu
ka?

toilettes publiques
kōshū benjo
tomate *tomato*
tort
Vous avez t.
Sore wa chigaimasu.
toujours *itsumo*
touriste *kankōkyaku*
tout droit *massugu*
Allez t.d.
Massugu itte kudasai.
traîneau *sori*
tramway *densha*
tranquille *shizuka*
transisteur radio
toranjisutā rajio
transpiration *ase*
travail d'artisan (j.)
mingei
tremblement de terre
jishin
très *taihen*
Très bien! *Taihen ii!*
triste *kanashii*
trois (choses) *mittsu*
trois (personnes) *sannin*
trois cents yen
sambyaku-en

troit de chaume *kayabuki-yane*	*kyūkyū-bako*
trousse de pansement	**tunnel** *tonneru*
	typhon *taifū*

— **U** —

un (chose) *hitotsu*	**un** (personne) *hitori*

— **V** —

vaccination (petite vérole) *shutō*	**verre** *koppu*
vaisseau *fune*	**vert** *midori*
valise *toranku*	**vestiaire** *kurōku*
vallée *tani*	**vêtements** (j.) *kimono*
vendeur *ten-in*	**vêtements** (e.) *yōfuku*
vendredi *Kinyōbi*	**vieux** (choses) *furui*
vent *kaze*	**vieux** (personnes) *toshiyori*
ventilateur éléctrique *sempūki*	**village** *mura*
vernis à ongles *tsume no enameru*	**ville** *toshi*
	ville (petite) *machi*
	vin *budōshu*

violet *murasaki*

visa *biza*

vitamine (pilule)
bitamin-jōzai

vite *hayaku*

vodka *uokka*

Voici mon adresse.
Kore ga watashi no jūsho desu.

voie ferrée *senro*

voir
Pourrais-je v. cela?
Sore o misete kudasai.

volcan *kazan*

Voleur! *Dorobō!*

vouloir
Que voulez-vous?
Nan deshō ka?

vouloir acheter
Je veux acheter une poupée japonaise.
Nihon ningyō o kaitai.

vouloir aller
Je veux aller au Ginza.
Ginza e ikitai.

vouloir visiter
Je veux visiter Kyoto.
Kyoto e ikitai.

vouloir voyager
Je veux voyager par monorail.
Monorēru ni noritai.

vous *anata*

voyage *ryokō*

vue *keshiki*

— W —

wagon (chemin de fer)
kyakusha

wagon de 1e classe
ittōsha

wagon de 2e classe
nitōsha

wagon-lits *shindaisha*

wagon-restaurant

W. C.

shokudōsha
W. C. *toire*
whisky *uisukī*
 double w. *daburu*

uisukī
whisky à l'eau
 haibōru

— Z —

zoo *dōbutsu-en*

DEUTSCH—JAPANISCH

JAPANISCHE AUSSPRACHE

Die japanische Aussprache ist verhältnismässig einfach. Das Wichtigste jedoch ist, 1) dass jede Silbe gleich stark betont wird—*Hiroshima (Hí-ró-shí-má)*; 2) dass es keine stummen Vokale gibt—*sake (sa-ke)*, und 3) dass, wenn zwei oder drei Vokale nebeneinander stehen, jeder klar ausgesprochen wird—*aoi (a-o-i)*.

VOKALE		KONSONANTEN	
		Nur Folgendes verdient Beachtung:	
a	Wasser	*ch*	Cello
e	wenn	*g*	gut
i	Kind	*j*	*Dsch*ungel
o	Sonne	*sh*	*Sch*al
u	Mutter		
ā	*Verdoppeln Sie den Laut bei diesen Vokalen.*		
ē (ei)	,,		
ī (ii)	,,		
ō	,,		
ū	,,		

— A —

Aal *unagi*

Abend *yūgata*
Guten A.! *Komban wa!*

Abendessen *yūshoku*

Abfahrtslauf (Ski)
kakkō kyōgi

Abfahrtszeit
shuppatsu-jikoku

Abflug *ririku*

Abflugszeit *shuppatsu-jikoku*

Abführmittel *gezai*

Abmeldezeit (Hotel)
chekku-auto taimu

Abszess *kanō*

Abzug (Foto) *purinto*

acht (in Bezug auf
Dinge) *yattsu*

acht (in Bezug auf Personen) *hachinin*

achthundert Yen
happyaku-en

Achtung! *Abunai!*

Adresse *jūsho*
Hier ist meine A.
*Kore ga watashi no
jūsho desu.*

Air Terminal *eā-
tāminaru*

à la carte *arakaruto*

Alkohol *arukōru*

alt (in Bezug auf Dinge)
furui

alt (in Bezug auf
Personen) *toshiyori*

Anblick *keshiki*

Andenken *miyage*

Ansichtskarte *ehagaki*

Ansteckung *kansen*

Antiquitäten *kottōhin*

Antiquitätenladen
kottōhin-ya

Anzug *sebiro*

Apfel *ringo*

April *Shigatsu*
Aquarell *suisaiga*
Arkade *ākēdo*
Arm *ude*
Armbanduhr *ude-dokei*
Arzt *isha*
  Rufen Sie bitte einen A.
  Isha o yonde kudasai.
  Wo kann ich einen A.
  finden? *Isha wa doko*
  desu ka?
Aschenbecher *haizara*
Aspirin *asupirin*
Auf Wiedersehen!
  Sayonara!
Aufzug *erebētā*

Auge *me*
Augenblick
  Einen A. bitte!
  Chotto matte kudasai!
Augentropfer *megusuri-*
  ire
Augenwasser *megusuri*
August *Hachigatsu*
Ausdünstung *ase*
Ausgang *deguchi*
Auskunftstelle *annaijo*
Ausländer *gaijin*
Auslandsgespräch
  kokusai denwa
Auster *kaki*
Auto *jidōsha*

— B —

Babysitter *komori*
Backenzahn *kyūshi*
Bad *furo*
  öffentliches B. (j.)
  sentō

  Sauna *sauna-buro*
  Schwitzb. *Toruko-buro*
Badetuch *basu-taoru*
Badezimmer *furoba*
  Wo ist das B.? (Hotel)

Yokushitsu wa doko desu ka?
Wo ist das B.? (zu Hause) *Furoba wa doko desu ka?*

Bahnhof *eki*

Bahnsteig *puratto hōmu*

Bahnsteigkarte *nyūjōken*

Bahnsteignummer *-bansen*

bald *mamonaku*

Balkonplatz *barukonī-seki*

Bambus *take*

Banane *banana*

Bar (Nachtlokal) *bā*

Bauer *nōfu*

Baum *ki*

Bedienen Sie sich bitte. *Go-jiyū ni.*

Bein *ashi*

belegtes Brot *sandoitchi*

Belichtungsmesser *roshutsu-kei*

Berg *yama*

Beruhigungsmittel *chinseizai*

Besuchskarte *meishi*

Betäubung (örtliche) *kyokubu masui*

Bett *betto*
Doppelb. *daburu betto*
Einzelb. *shinguru betto*

Bettuch *shītsu*

Beule *kobu*

Beutel *saifu*

Bier *bīru*
eine Flasche B. *bīru ippon*

billig *yasui*

Birne (j.) *nashi*

Bitte. (Nehmen Sie es. Gehen Sie voraus.) *Dōzo.*

Bitte. (Bringen Sie mir. Geben Sie mir.) *Kudasai.*

Bitte. (Helfen Sie mir. Bedienen Sie mich.) *O-negai shimasu.*

Bitte schön. *Dō-itashimashite.*

Blase (Pustel) *mizubukure*

blau *burū*
Bleistift *empitsu*
Blinddarmentzündung
  mōchōen
Blitzlicht *furasshu*
Blume *hana*
Blumenarrangieren (j.)
  ikebana
Blumenhändler *hanaya*
Blumenkohl *karifurawā*
Blutdruck *ketsuatsu*
Bobbahn *bobbu surē kōsu*
Bobschlitten *bobbu surē*
Bohnenkeime *moyashi*
Botanischer Garten
  shokubutsu-en
Botschaft *taishikan*
braun *chairo*
Brausebad *shawā*
Brechreiz *hakike*
breit *hiroi*
Brief *tegami*

Briefkasten *posuto*
Briefmarke *kitte*
Brille *megane*
Brokat *burokēdo*
Bronchitis *kikanshi-en*
Bronze *seidō*
Brot *pan*
Brücke *hashi*
Bruder (Ihr älterer)
  o-niisan
Bruder (Ihr jüngerer)
  otōtosan
Bruder (mein älterer)
  ani
Bruder (mein jüngerer)
  otōto
Buchhandlung *hon-ya*
Bucht *wan*
Bügeleisen *airon*
Bummelzug *futsū ressha*
Butter *batā*

— C —

Chirurg *geka-i*
Chrysantheme *kiku*

Cornflakes *kōnfurēkusu*

— D —

da *asoko*
Damen-Toilette
  o-tearai
  Wo ist die T.? *O-tearai*
  wa doko desu ka?
Danke! *Arigatō!*
Danke. (Ich habe genug.)
  Kekkō desu.
Danke schön.
  Arigatō gozaimasu.
dasjenige *sore*
dasselbe *onaji*
Dattelpflaume *kaki*
Denkmal *kinenhi*

Deodorant (Armhöhle)
  asedome
derselbe *onaji*
Deutsch (Sprache)
  Doitsugo
Deutsche(r) *Doitsu-jin*
Deutsche Botschaft
  Doitsu Taishikan
  Wo ist die D. B.?
  Doitsu Taishikan wa
  doko desu ka?
Deutsches Konsulat
  Doitsu Ryōjikan
  Wo ist das D. K.?

95

*Doitsu Ryōjikan wa
doko desu ka?*
Deutschland *Doitsu*
Dezember *Jūnigatsu*
Diapositiv *suraido*
dick *futotta*
Dieb! *Dorobō!*
Dienstag *Kayōbi*
dieselbe *onaji*
diesjenige *kore*
Direktor (Hotel)
shihainin
Dolmetscher *tsūyaku*
Donnerstag *Mokuyōbi*
Doppelbett *daburu betto*
**doppelkohlensaures
Natron** *jūsō*

Doppelzimmer (Hotel)
daburu rūmu
Dorf *mura*
Dosenöffner *kan-kiri*
drei (in Bezug auf
Dinge) *mittsu*
drei (in Bezug auf
Personen) *sannin*
dreihundert Yen
sambyaku-en
Drogerie *kusuriya*
Druck (j.) *hanga*
Durchfall *geri*
durstig
Ich bin d.
Nodo ga kawakimashita.
Düsenflieger *jettoki*

— **E** —

Ehefrau (Ihre) *okusan*
Ehefrau (meine) *tsuma*
Ei *tamago*
hart gekochtes E.
yude-tamago

rohes E. *nama-tamago*
Rühre. *iri-tamago*
Spiegele. *medama yaki*
verlorenes E. *otoshi-
tamago*

weich gekochtes E.
hanjuku-tamago

ein (in Bezug auf Dinge)
hitotsu

ein (in Bezug auf
Personen) *hitori*

eine Million Yen
hyakuman-en

**Einen Augenblick
bitte!** *Chotto matte
kudasai!*

Einen Moment bitte!
Chotto matte kudasai!

einfache Fahrkarte
katamichi kippu

Eingang *iriguchi*

Eingepökeltes (j.
Gemüse) *tsukemono*

Einkäufe machen
kaimono

Einlauf *kanchō*

einmal *ichido*

Einreibemittel
nuri-gusuri

Einschreibebrief
kakitome

Eintrittsgeld *nyūjōryō*

Einwanderungs-

beamter *imin kan*

Einwanderungsbüro
Nyūkoku Kanri-kyoku

Einzelbett *shinguru betto*

Einzelbetten *tsuin-betto*

Einzelzimmer (Hotel)
shinguru rūmu

Eis *kōri*

Eis(krem) *aisukurīmu*

Eisbahn *sukēto-jō*

Eistee *aisu-tī*

Eiswasser *aisu-uōtā*

elektrischer Rasierapparat *denki kamisori*

elektrischer Ventilator
sempūki

Elfenbein *zōge*

eng *semai*

Englisch
Sprechen Sie E.?
Eigo o hanashimasu ka?

Enkel (Fuss) *ashikubi*

Entschuldigen Sie!
Gomen nasai!

Erbsen *mame*

Erdbeben *jishin*

Erdbeeren *ichigo*

Erdgeschoss *ikkai*

97

Erdnuss *pīnatsu*
Erkältung *kaze*
erster Stock *nikai*

Esslöffel *ōsaji*
Esstäbchen *hashi*
etwas *nani ka*

— F —

Fächer (j. Papier) *sensu*
Fahren Sie bitte lang-
    samer. *Motto yukkuri
    hashitte kudasai.*
Fahrgeld *ryōkin*
    halber Preis *hangaku*
Fahrkarte *kippu*
    einfache F. *katamichi
    kippu*
    Rückf. *ōfuku kippu*
Fahrrad *jitensha*
Fahrstuhl *erebētā*
falsch
    Das ist f.
    Sore wa chigaimasu.
falsche Nummer
    (Telefon) *bangō chigai*
Farbfilm *karā-firumu*
Farbspülung (Haar)

karā rinsu
Februar *Nigatsu*
Feiertag *kyūjitsu*
Feldstecher *sōgankyō*
Fernsehen *terebi*
Fernsehkanal *terebi
    channeru*
Fernsprecher *denwa*
    Wo ist der F.?
    *Denwa wa doko desu
    ka?*
fertig
    Ich bin f.
    Jumbi ga dekimashita.
    Ich bin noch nicht f.
    Mada desu.
    Sind Sie f.?
    Jumbi wa ii desu ka?
    Wann wird es f. sein?

Itsu dekimasu ka?
feucht *shikki ga ōi*
Feuer! *Kaji!*
Feuerstein *ishi*
Feuerzeug *raitā*
Feuerzeugbenzin
  raitā-eki
Fieber *netsu*
Figurenlaufen *figyā*
  sukēto
Figurenläufer *figyā*
  sukētā
Film (Rolle) *firumu*
  Farbf. *karā-firumu*
  schwarz-weiss F.
  shirokuro firumu
Film (Ton) *eiga*
Filmkamera *mūbī*
  kamera
Finger *yubi*
Fingernagel *yubi no*
  tsume
Fisch *sakana*
  roher F. (j. essbar)
  sashimi
Fischer *ryōshi*
Flasche *bin*
Flaschenöffner *sen-nuki*

Flughafen *kūkō*
Flugkarte *kippu*
Flugnummer *furaito*
  nambā
Flugzeug *hikōki*
Fluss *kawa*
Fotogeschäft *kameraya*
Fotografie *shashin*
Frau *onna no hito*
Frau (Anrede) *-san*
Frauenarzt *fujinka*
Fräulein (Anrede) *-san*
frei
  Ist dieser Platz f.?
  Kono seki wa aite
  imasu ka?
Freitag *Kinyōbi*
freuen
  Es freut mich, Sie
  kennen zu lernen.
  Hajimemashite. Dōzo
  yoroshiku.
Freund *tomodachi*
Friseur (Geschäft) *biyōin*
Friseur *tokoya*
Friseuse *biyōshi*
Frost *shimo*
früh *hayai*

Frühling *haru*
Früstück *chōshoku*
Fundbüro
  ishitsu-butsu atsukaijo
fünf (in Bezug auf
  Dinge) *itsutsu*
fünf (in Bezug auf
  Personen) *gonin*

fünfhundert Yen
  gohyaku-en
fünftausend Yen
  gosen-en
fünf Yen *go-en*
fünfzig Yen *gojū-en*
Furunkel *dekimono*
Fuss *ashi*

— **G** —

Gabel *hōku*
Garderobe *kurōku*
Garnele *ebi*
Garten *niwa*
  Blumeng. *hanazono*
  japanischer G.
  Nihon tei-en
  Steing. (j.) *sekitei*
Gasthof (j.) *ryokan*
Gatte (Ihr) *go-shujin*
Gatte (mein) *shujin*
Gattin (Ihre) *okusan*
Gattin (meine) *tsuma*
Gedeck *kabā-chaji*

gefroren *reitō*
gehen
  Mir geht's gut, danke.
  Genki desu, arigatō.
  Wie geht's?
  Ikaga desu ka?
gelb *kiiro*
Geld *o-kane*
Gelee *zerī*
Geleise *senro*
Gemäldegallerie *garō*
Gemüse *yasai*
genug
  Das ist g., danke.

*Sore de kekkō desu,
arigatō.*
Ich habe g. *Kekkō desu.*
Gepäck *tenimotsu*
Gepäckschein
tenimotsu no chikki
Gepäckträger *akabō*
Gepäckzuschlag
chōka-tenimotsu
gerade aus *massugu*
Gehen Sie g. a.
Massugu itte kudasai.
Gerstenkorn (am Auge)
monomorai
Geschäftsstrasse
(Touristen) *ākēdo*
Geschenk *okurimono*
Gesicht *kao*
Gesichtspuder *kona
oshiroi*
gestern *kinō*
Gesundheitsschein
kenkō shindansho
gewiss
Sind Sie ganz g.?
Tashika desu ka?
glauben
Ich g. es. *Sō omoimasu.*

Ich g. es nicht.
Sō omoimasen.
glücklich *shiawase*
Glückwunsch
Herzlichen Glück-
wunsch! *O-medetō
gozaimasu!*
Gold *kin*
Grippe *infuruenza*
gross (generell) *ōkii*
gross (hoch) *takai*
Grösse (Kleidung) *saizu*
grüne Bohnen *saya-
ingen*
grüner Salt *retasu*
Gurgelwasser *ugai*
Gurt (Flugzeug)
zaseki-beruto
gut *ii*
Mir geht's g.
Genki desu.
Guten Abend!
Komban wa!
Gute Nacht!
O-yasumi nasai!
Guten Morgen!
O-hayō gozaimasu!
Guten Tag! (früh)

101

O-hayō gozaimasu!
Guten Tag! (mittags,

nachmittags)
Konnichi wa!

— H —

Haar (Kopf) *kami no ke*
Haarbürste *hea-burashi*
Haarklemme *hea-pin*
Haarnadel *hea-pin*
Haarschnitt *sampatsu*
Haarspray *hea-supurē*
Haarteil *hea-pīsu*
Haarwickel *amikarā*
Haferbrei *ōto mīru*
halber Preis *hangaku*
Hallo! (am
   Fernsprecher) *Moshi,
   moshi!*
Halsschmerzen
   nodo no itami
Halten Sie bitte hier.
   Koko de ii desu.
Hand *te*
Handcreme *hando-
   rōshon*

handgemacht *tesei*
Handgepäck *tenimotsu*
Handkoffer *toranku*
Handschuhe *tebukuro*
Handtasche (Damen)
   hando-baggu
Handtuch *taoru*
   heisses H. (im
   Restaurant gereicht)
   o-shibori
hart gekochtes Ei
   yude-tamago
hässlich *minikui*
Haut (Mensch) *hifu*
Haut (Tier) *kawa*
Hautausschlag
   jimmashin
Heftpflaster *bansōkō*
Heimweh *hōmushikku*
heiser *shagare-goe*

102

heiss *atsui*
heisses Handtuch (im Restaurant gereicht) *o-shibori*
heisses Wasser *o-yu*
Herbst *aki*
Herr (Anrede) *-san*
Herren-Toilette *tearai*
Wo ist die T.?
Tearai wa doko desu ka?
Herr Ober!
Chotto o-negai shimasu!
Heufieber *kafun netsu*
heute *kyō*
heute Abend *komban*
hier *koko ni*
Hier ist meine Adresse. *Kore ga watashi no jūsho desu.*
Highball *haibōru*
Hilfe
Sie waren mir eine grosse H.
O-sewa-sama deshita.
Hilfe! *Tasukete!*
Himmel *sora*

Hinauf? (zu dem Fahrstuhlführer) *Ue?*
Hinunter? (zu dem Fahrstuhlführer) *Shita?*
Histamin (Pille) *kō-hisutamin*
Hochhaus *matenrō*
Holzdruck (j.) *hanga*
Holzschuhe (j.) *geta*
Hotel (j.) *ryokan*
Hotel (w.) *hoteru*
Hotelpage *beru bōi*
hübsch *kirei*
Hühnerauge *tako*
Hühnerfleisch *keiniku*
hunderttausend Yen *jūman-en*
hundert Yen *hyaku-en*
hungrig
Ich bin h.
O-naka ga sukimashita.
Husten *seki*
Hustenbonbon *sekidome doroppu*
Hut *bōshi*

103

— I —

ich *watashi*
Imbiss *sunakku*
Imbisspäckchen (j.,
am Bahnsteig verkauft)
ekiben
immer *itsumo*
Impfung *shutō*
Impfschein *yobō chūsha
shōmeisho*
Insekt *mushi*

Insel *shima*
interessant *omoshiroi*
Das ist i.
Omoshiroi desu.
**internationale
Postanweisung**
gaikoku yūbin-gawase
Iris (Schwertlilie)
ayame
Irrtum *machigai*

— J —

Ja. *Hai.*
Jade *hisui*
Jahr *toshi*
Jamswurzel (j.)
satsuma-imo
Januar *Ichigatsu*

Japan *Nippon*
Japan Air Lines (**JAL**)
Nihon Kōkū
Japaner(in) *Nihon-jin*
Japanisch (Sprache)
Nihongo

japanisch (Ware)
  Nihon sei
**Japan National
  Railways** (JNR)
  Kokutetsu
**Japan Travel Bureau
  (JTB)** *Nihon Kōtsū
  Kōsha*

jetzt *ima*
Jod *yōdochinki*
Jugendherberge
  yūsu-hosuteru
Juli *Shichigatsu*
jung *wakai*
Juni *Rokugatsu*
Juwelier *hōseki-ten*

— K —

Kaffee *kōhī*
  eine Tasse K.
  kōhī ippai
  schwarzer K.
  burakku-kōhī
Kaffe mit Sahne
  miruku iri kōhī
Kaiser (j.) *Tennō*
Kaiserin (j.) *Kōgōheika*
kalt (in Bezug auf Personen und Wetter)
  samui
kalt (in Bezug auf
  Dinge) *tsumetai*

kaltes Wasser *tsumetai
  mizu*
Kamelie *tsubaki*
Kamera *kamera*
  Filmk. *mūbī kamera*
Kamerageschäft
  kameraya
Kamm *kushi*
Kapsel (Pille) *kapuseru*
Karotte *ninjin*
Karpfen *koi*
Karpfen (fliegender,
  Knabenfest) *koinobori*
Kartoffel *jagaimo*

Jamswurzel (j.)
  satsuma-imo
Käse chīzu
Kassierer suitō-gakari
Kater (nach Alkohol)
  futsuka-yoi
Kaugummi chuīn-gamu
Kehlkopfentzündung
  kōtōen
Kellergeschoss
  chikashitsu
Kellner kyūji
  Oberk. chīfu-uētā
Kellnerin uētoresu
Kellnerin!
  Chotto o-negai shimasu!
Kilo(gramm)
  kiro(guramu)
Kilometer kiro(mētoru)
Kind kodomo
Kino eigakan
Kirschblüten
  sakura no hana
Kleenex (j.) chirigami
Kleenex (w.)
  kurīnekkusu
Kleid (w.) doresu
Kleiderbügel hangā

Kleidung (j.) kimono
Kleidung (w.) yōfuku
klein chiisai
kleines Kind akambō
Kleingeld kozeni
Klimaanlage reibō
Klistierspritze
  kanchōki
Klosettpapier (j.)
  chirigami
Klosettpapier (w.)
  toiretto-pēpā
Knabe otoko no ko
Knie hiza
Kohl kyabetsu
Koje (Zug) dan-betto
  obere K. jōdan betto
  untere K. gedan betto
Konfitüre jamu
Konsulat ryōjikan
Kopf atama
Kopfkissen makura
Kopfmassage
  atama no massāji
Korkenzieher
  koruku-nuki
kostenlos tada
Krabbe kani

Krämpfe *keiren*
krank *byōki*
  Ich fühle mich k.
  Kibun ga warui desu.
Krankenhaus *byōin*
Krebs (Schalentier) *ebi*
Kreditkarte *kurejitto-*

kādo
Kuchen *kēki*
Kugelfisch (j.
  Delikatesse) *fugu*
Kugelschreiber *bōru*
pen
kurz *mijikai*

— L —

Lachs *sake*
lackierte Ware *shikki*
Laden (Geschäft) *mise*
Landkarte *chizu*
Landung (Flugzeug)
  chakuriku
lang (Länge) *nagai*
lang (Zeit) *nagai aida*
langsam *yukkuri*
langsamer
  Fahren Sie bitte l.
  Motto yukkuri hashitte
  kudasai.
  Sprechen Sie bitte l.
  Motto yukkuri hana-

shite kudasai.
Laterne (j. Metall) *tōrō*
Laterne (j. Papier)
  chōchin
Laterne (j. Stein)
  ishi-dōrō
laut *yakamashii*
Leder *kawa*
Lehrer *sensei*
leicht *yasashii*
leid tun
  Es tut mir leid.
  O-ki no doku desu.
Leiter *gaido*
Leukoplast *bansōkō*

Lied

Lied *uta*	**los**
Lila *murasaki*	Was ist l.?
links *hidari*	*Dō shimashita ka?*
Links abbiegen bitte.	**Luftkrankheit** *hikōki-yoi*
Hidari e magatte	**Luftpost** *kōkūbin*
kudasai.	mit (per) L. *kōkūbin de*
Lippenstift *kuchibeni*	**Luftpostbrief** *kōkūbin*
Liter *rittoru*	**Luftpostmarke**
Lockenwickel *amikarā*	*kōkūbin kitte*
Löffel *supūn*	**Luftverkehrsbüro**
Essl. *osaji*	*kōkū-gaisha*
Suppenl. *sūpu-supūn*	**Luftverkehrslinie**
Teel. *chasaji*	*kōkūro*

— **M** —

Mach schnell! *Hayaku!*	**Maler** (Künstler) *gaka*
Mädchen *onna no ko*	**manchmal** *toki-doki*
Magazin *zasshi*	**Mandarine** *mikan*
Magenschmerzen *i no*	**Mandelentzündung**
itami	*hentōsen-en*
Magenverstimmung	**Maniküre** *manikyua*
fushōka	**Maniküristin**
Mahlzeit *shokuji*	*manikyua-shi*
Mai *Gogatsu*	**Mann** *otoko no hito*

Mantel *kōto*
Martini *mātīnī*
März *Sangatsu*
Massage *massāji*
  Kopfm.
  atama no massāji
Masseur *otoko-amma*
Masseuse *onna-amma*
Mayonnaise *mayonēzu*
Medizin *kusuri*
Meer *umi*
Melone *meron*
Messe (Ausstellung)
  hakurankai
Messingware *shinchū-
  zaiku*
Meter *mētoru*
Milch *miruku*
  ein Glas M.
  miruku ippai
Million Yen (eine)
  hyakuman-en
Mineralöl *mineraru oiru*
Mineralwasser
  tansansui
Minute *fun*
Mittag *hiru*
Mittagessen *chūshoku*

Mitternacht *mayonaka*
Mittwoch *Suiyōbi*
mögen
  Ich mag es. *Suki desu.*
  Ich mag es nicht.
  Kirai desu.
  Ich möchte Kyoto be-
  suchen. *Kyōto e ikitai.*
  Ich möchte mit dem
  Monorail fahren.
  Monorēru ni noritai.
  Ich möchte zur
  Ginza gehen.
  Ginza e ikitai.
  Ich möchte eine japa-
  nische Puppe kaufen.
  Nihon ningyō o kaitai.
  Mögen Sie es?
  Suki desu ka?
Moment
  Einen M. bitte!
  Chotto matte kudasai!
Monat *tsuki*
Montag *Getsuyōbi*
Morgen *asa*
  Guten M.!
  O-hayō gozaimasu!
morgen *ashita*

Motorrad *ōtobai*
müde
  Ich bin m.
  Tsukaremashita.
Mund *kuchi*

Museum *hakubutsukan*
Musik *ongaku*
Mutter (Ihre) *o-kāsan*
Mutter (meine) *haha*

— N —

Nachmittag *gogo*
Nachrichten *nyūzu*
Nacht *yoru*
  Gute N.!
  O-yasumi nasai!
Nachtisch *dezāto*
Nachtklub *naito-kurabu*
Nagelfeile *tsume-yasuri*
Nagellack
  tsume no enameru
Nagellackentferner
  jokō-eki
nahe *chikai*
Name *namae*
Nase *hana*
Nasenbluten *hanaji*
Nasentropfen

  hanagusuri
nass *nureta*
Nationalpark *kokuritsu-kōen*
Nebel *kiri*
Negativ (Foto) *nega*
Nein! (Tun Sie das
  nicht!) *Dame!*
Nein. (Ich mag es
  nicht.) *Kirai desu.*
Nein. (Das ist falsch.)
  Chigaimasu.
nervös *shinkeishitsu*
nett *ii*
neu *atarashii*
neun (in Bezug auf
  Dinge) *kokonotsu*

neun (in Bezug auf Personen) *kunin*
neunhundert Yen *kyū-hyaku-en*
nichts *nanimo*
niedrig *hikui*
noch etwas *motto*
Norden *kita*
November *Jūichigatsu*
Novokain *nobokain*

Nudeln (j.) *udon, soba*
Nummer *bangō*
　Bahnsteign. *-bansen*
　Flugn. *furaito nambā*
　Platzn. *zaseki-bangō*
　Telefonn. *denwa-bangō*
　Zimmern. *heya-bangō*
Nylonstrümpfe
　sutokkingu

— O —

obere Koje (Zug)
　jōdan betto
Oberkellner *chīfu-uētā*
Obst *kudamono*
Obstsaft *furūtsu-jūsu*
öffnen
　Um wieviel Uhr öffnet
　es?
　Nanji ni akimasu ka?
öffentliches Bad (j.)
　sentō
öffentliche Toilette

　kōshū benjo
Ohr *mimi*
Ohrenschmerzen
　mimi no itami
O. K.! *Okē!*
Oktober *Jūgatsu*
Ölgemälde *abura-e*
Omelett *omuretsu*
Omnibus *basu*
　Tourenbus *kankō-basu*
Omnibusfahrer
　basu no untenshu

111

Onkel (Ihr) *ojisan*
Onkel (mein) *oji*
Operation (ärztliche)
shujutsu
Orange *orenji*
Mandarine *mikan*
Orangensaft *orenji-jūsu*
Orchesterplatz
ōkesutora bokkusu

Ordnung
Alles ist in O.
Kamaimasen.
Orientale *Tōyōjin*
örtliche Betäubung
kyokubu masui
Osten *higashi*
Ozean *taiyō*

— P —

Pagode *tō*
Paket Zigaretten
tabako hitohako
Papier *kami*
handgemachtes P. (j.)
washi
Klosettp. (j.) *chirigami*
Klosettp. (w.)
toiretto-pēpā
Schreibp. *binsen*
Park *kōen*
Parterre *ikkai*
Pasteten *okashi*

Penicillin *penishirin*
Perle *shinju*
Perlenkette
shinju no nekkuresu
Perücke *katsura*
Pfeffer *koshō*
Pfefferstreuer *koshō-ire*
Pfeife *paipu*
Pfeifentabak
paipu-tabako
Pferd *uma*
Pfirsich *momo*
Pflaumensaft

puramu-jūsu
Pflegerin (für Kranke) *kangofu*
Pille *gan-yaku*
Pilot (Flugzeug) *pairotto*
Platz (Theater, Zug, usf.) *seki*
Platzanweiser *annai-nin*
Platznummer *zaseki-bangō*
Plombe (Zahn) *mushiba no tsumemono*
Polizeiwache *keisatsusho*
Polizist *keikan*

Rufen Sie bitte einen P. *Keikan o yonde kudasai.*
Porzellan *tōki*
Porzellanladen *tōkiya*
Postamt *yūbinkyoku*
postlagernde Briefe *kyoku-dome*
Preis *nedan*
Projektor (Film) *eishaki*
Projektor (Diapositiv) *gentōki*
Prosit! *Kampai!*
Psychiater *seishinka-i*
Pudding *purin*
Puppe (j.) *ningyō*

— Q —

Quetschung *uchimi* | **Quittung** *uketori*

113

— R —

Radio *rajio*

Rasierklinge
kamisori no ha

Rasierkrem
shēbingu kurīmu

Rasierpinsel
higesori burashi

Rechenbrett *soroban*

Rechnung (Laden)
seikyūsho

Rechnung (Restaurant, Bar) *kanjō*

rechts *migi*

Rechts abbiegen, bitte.
Migi e magatte kudasai.

Regen *ame*

Regenguss *bōfū-u*

Regenmantel *rēnkōto*

Regenschirm (j. Papier)
bangasa

Regenschirm (w.)
ama-gasa

Regenzeit *tsuyu*

Reinigung *kurīninguya*

Reis (gekocht) *gohan*

Reis (ungekocht) *kome*

Reisbiskuit (j.) *sembei*

Reise *ryokō*

Reisebüro *kōtsū-kōsha*

Reiseführer *annai-sho*

Reisehandbuch
ryokō-annai

Reisepass *pasupōto*

Reiseroute *ryotei*

Reisescheck
toraberā-chekku

Reisfeld *tambo*

Reissverschluss *jippā*

Rennbahn (Pferde)
keibajō

reservierter Platz
shitei-seki

reservierter Tisch
yoyaku-seki

Reservierung *yoyaku*
Ich habe reservieren
lassen. *Watashi wa
yoyaku o shite imasu.*
Restaurant (j.) *ryōriya*
Restaurant (w.)
resutoran
Rettich (j.) *daikon*
Revue (Theater) *rebyū*
richtig
Das ist r. *Sō desu.*
Richtung
In welcher R. ist es?
*Dochira no hōkō desu
ka?*
roher Fisch (j. essbar)
sashimi
rohes Ei *nama-tamago*
Rohseide (Stoff)
rō shiruku
Rollbild (j. hängend)

kakemono
Rolltreppe *esukarētā*
Röntgenaufnahme
rentogen
Rose *bara*
rot *aka*
Rücken (Körper)
senaka
Rückfahrkarte *ōfuku
kippu*
**Rufen Sie bitte einen
Arzt (Polizist).**
*Isha (keikan) o yonde
kudasai.*
**Rufen Sie bitte ein
Taxi.** *Takushī o yonde
kudasai.*
ruhig *shizuka*
Rührei *iri-tamago*
rund *marui*

115

— S —

Saft *jūsu*

Sahne *kurīmu*
  Schlags. *nama kurīmu*

Salat *sarada*

Salbe *nuri-gusuri*

Salz *shio*

Salzfass *shio-ire*

Salzwasser *shio-mizu*

Samstag *Doyōbi*

Sand *suna*

Sauna *sauna-buro*

Schachtel Zigarren
  hamaki hitohako

Schale *kawa*

Schallplatte *rekōdo*

Schalterfenster
  mado-guchi

scharf (Messer, usf.)
  surudoi

Schärpe (j.) *obi*

Schauspiel *shibai*

Schauspielhaus *gekijō*

Schenkwirt *bāten*

Schere *hasami*

Schiebetür (j. halb-
durchsichtiges Papier)
  shōji

Schiff *fune*

Schinken *hamu*

Schinken mit Ei
  hamu-eggu

Schlafdecke *mōfu*

Schlaflosigkeit
  fuminsho

Schlafmittel *suimin-
yaku*

Schlafwagen
  shindaisha

Schlafzimmer
  shinshitsu

Schlagsahne *nama
kurīmu*

schlecht *warui*

schliessen

Um wieviel Uhr
schliesst es? *Nanji ni
shimarimasu ka?*

Schlitten *sori*

Schlittschuhe *aisu
sukēto*

Schlittschuhlaufen
aisu sukēto

Schlittschuhläufer
sukētā

Schloss (Burg) *shiro*

Schlüssel *kagi*

Schmerz *itami*

Schmirgelfeile
tsume yasuri

Schnee *yuki*

Schneesturm *fubuki*

schnell *hayaku*

Schnellzug *kyūkō*

Schokolade *chokorēto
bā*

schottischer Whisky
Sukotchi

Schreiben Sie es bitte.
Sore o kaite kudasai.

Schreibpapier *binsen*

Schrein (Schintoismus)
jinja

Schuhe *kutsu*

Schuhe putzen
kutsu migaki

Schüssel *sara*

schwarz *kuro*

schwarzer Kaffee
burakku-kōhī

schwarz-weiss Film
shirokuro firumu

Schweinefleisch
butaniku

Schweineschnitzel
pōku katsuretsu

Schwester (Ihre ältere)
o-nēsan

Schwester (Ihre
jüngere) *imōto-san*

Schwester (meine
ältere) *ane*

Schwester (meine
jüngere) *imōto*

Schwimmbecken *pūru*

Schwitzbad *Toruko-
buro*

sechs (in Bezug auf
Dinge) *muttsu*

sechs (in Bezug auf
Personen) *rokunin*

117

sechshundert Yen
roppyaku-en

See (der) *mizu-umi*

See (die) *umi*

Seeigel (essbar) *uni*

Seespeise *gyokairui*

Seetang (essbar) *nori*

sehen
Kann ich das s.?
Sore o misete kudasai.

Sehen Sie mal!
Minasai!

sehr *taihen*

Sehr gut! *Taihen ii!*

Seide (Stoff) *kinu*

Seife *sekken*

Sekt *shampen*

Sekunde *byō*

Sellerie *serorī*

Semmel *rōru-pan*

Senf *karashi*

Separatrechnung bitte.
*Betsubetsu ni kanjō o
shite kudasai.*

September *Kugatsu*

Serviette *nafukin*

Sicherheitsgurt
anzen beruto

Sicherheitsnadel
anzen-pin

Sie *anata*

sieben (in Bezug auf
Dinge) *nanatsu*

sieben (in Bezug auf
Personen) *shichinin*

siebenhundert Yen
nanahyaku-en

Silber *gin*

Ski *sukī*

Skibindung *sukī
baindingu*

Skigeländelauf *dankō
kyōsō*

Skilaufen *sukī*

Skiläufer *sukīyā*

Skilift *sukī rifuto*

Skistieffel *sukī-gutsu*

Skistöcke *sukī sutokku*

Slalom *kaiten*

Sohn (ihr) *musuko-san*

Sohn (mein) *musuko*

Sommer *natsu*

Sommerurlaubsort
hishochi

Sonnabend *Doyōbi*

Sonne *taiyō*

Sonnenbrand *hiyake*

Sonnenbrille *sangurasu*

Sonnenöl *hiyake-oiru*

Sonnenschein *nikkō*

Sonnenschirm *higasa*

Sonntag *Nichiyōbi*

Soya-Sosse *shōyu*

spanisches Rohr *tō*

Spass
Ich habe viel S. gehabt.
Totemo tanoshikatta.
Viel S.!
Tanoshiku dōzo!

spät *osoi*

Speck *bēkon*

Speck mit Ei *bēkon to tamago*

Speise *tabemono*

Speisekarte *menyū*

Speisevergiftung *shoku-chūdoku*

Speisewagen *shokudōsha*

Speisezimmer *shokudō*

Spiegel *kagami*

Spiegelei *medama yaki*

Spielkarten *torampu hito kumi*

Spielzeug *omocha*

Spirituosengeschäft *sakaya*

Sport *supōtsu*

Sprechen Sie bitte langsamer. *Motto yukkuri hanashite kudasai.*

Sprechen Sie English? *Eigo o hanashimasu ka?*

Spritze (Einspritzung) *chūsha*

Sprungschanze *sukī jampu*

Stadt *toshi*

Stadt (kleine) *machi*

Statue *zō*

Steak *sutēki*

Stecknadel *machi-bari*

Steingarten (j.) *sekitei*

Stern *hoshi*

steuerfrei *menzei*

Stewardess (Flugzeug) *suchūwadesu*

Stiller Ozean *Taiheiyō*

Strasse *-dōri*

Strassenbahn *densha*

119

Streichholz *matchi*
Strohdach *kayabuki-yane*
Strohmatte (j.) *tatami*
Student *seito*
Stunde (eine) *ichijikan*
suchen
  Ich suche —.
  — *o sagashite imasu.*
Süden *minami*

Suppe (j.)
  klare S. *suimono*
  Miso-S. (mit Bohnen-paste) *misoshiru*
Suppe (w.) *sūpu*
Suppenlöffel *sūpu-supūn*
Suppenteller *sūpu-zara*
Süssigkeiten *kyandē*
Süsstoff *sakkarin*

— T —

Tabak *tabako*
Tabak für Pfeife
  paipu-tabako
Tabaksbeutel *tabako-ire*
Tafel Schokolade
  chokorēto bā
Tag *hi*
  Es ist ein schlechter T.
  Warui tenki desu.
  Es ist ein schöner T.
  Ii tenki desu.
  Guten T.! (Guten

Morgen!) *O-hayō gozaimasu!*
  Guten T.! (mittags, nachmittags) *Konnichi wa!*
Taifun *taifū*
Tal *tani*
Tante (Ihre) *obasan*
Tante (meine) *oba*
Tasche *poketto*
Tasse *kappu*
tausend Yen *sen-en*

Taxi *takushī*
Rufen Sie bitte ein T.
*Takushī o yonde
kudasai.*

Taxifahrer
takushī no untenshu

Tee (j. grüner) *o-cha*

Tee (w. schwarzer) *kōcha*
Eist. *aisu-tī*

Teelöffel *chasaji*

Teetasse (j.) *chawan*

Teetasse (w.) *kōcha-
jawan*

Teezeremonie (j.)
chanoyu

Telefonistin *kōkanshu*

Telefonnummer
denwa-bangō

Telegrafenamt
denshin-kyoku

Telegramm *dempō*
Wo kann ich ein T.
absenden? *Dempō wa
doko de utemasu ka?*

Teller *sara*

Tempel (Buddhismus)
tera

Tesafilm *sero-tēpu*

teuer *takai*
Es ist zu t.
Taka-sugimasu.

Theater
(Schauspielhaus)
gekijō

Theaterkasse *kippu-
uriba*

Thunfisch *maguro*

tief *fukai*

Tier *dōbutsu*

Tintenfisch *ika*

Toast *tōsuto*

Tochter (Ihre) *o-jōsan*

Tochter (meine) *musume*

Toilette *tearai*
öffentliche T.
kōshū benjo

Tomate *tomato*

Tomatenketchup
kechappu

Tomatensaft *tomato-
jūsu*

Tonbandgerät *tēpu-
rekōdā*

Töpferware *yakimono*

Torbogen (Schinto-
Schrein) *torii*

Tourenbus *kankō basu*
Tourist *kankōkyaku*
Träger (Gepäck) *akabō*
Transistor-Radio
　toranjisutā rajio
traurig *kanashii*
Treppe *kaidan*

Trinkglas *koppu*
Trinkwasser *nomi mizu*
trocken *kansō*
Trockenpflaume
　(geschmorte) *nikomi-*
　puramu
Tunnel *tonneru*

— U —

Übergewicht (Gepäck)
　chōka-tenimotsu
Überseetelegramm
　kokusai dempō
　Wo kann ich ein Ü.
　absenden? *Kokusai*
　dempō wa doko de
　utemasu ka?
Uhr (Zeit) *-ji*
　Wieviel U. ist es?
　Nanji desu ka?
Umschlag *fūtō*

und *to*
Unfall *jiko*
untere Koje (Zug)
　gedan betto
Untergrundbahn
　chikatetsu
Untergrundbahnhof
　chikatetsu no eki
Untertasse *kozara*
Urlaubsort *hoyō*
　Sommeru. *hishochi*
　Winteru. *sukī-jō*

— V —

Vater (Ihr) *o-tōsan*
Vater (mein) *chichi*
Verabredung *yakusoku*
Verband (medizinisch)
  hōtai
Verbandskasten
  kyūkyū-bako
Vergnügungspark
  yūenchi
verirren
  Ich habe mich verirrt.
  Michi ni mayoimashita.
Verkäufer(in) *ten-in*
Verkehrszeichen
  kōtsū-shingō
verlaufen
  Ich habe mich
  verlaufen. *Michi ni*
  mayoimashita.
verletzt *kega o shita*
verlorenes Ei
  otoshi-tamago

Verrenkung *nenza*
verstehen
  Ich verstehe.
  Wakarimashita.
  Ich verstehe nicht.
  Wakarimasen.
  Verstehen Sie?
  Wakarimasu ka?
Verstopfung *bempi*
Verzeihen Sie!
  Gomen nasai!
Vetter *itoko*
viel(e) *takusan*
Viel Glück! *Kōun o*
  inoru!
vielleicht *tabun*
viel Spass
  Ich habe v. S. gehabt.
  Totemo tanoshikatta.
  V. S.! *Tanoshiku dōzo!*
vier (in Bezug auf
  Dinge) *yottsu*

vier (in Bezug auf
Personen) *yonin*
viereckig *shikaku*
vierhundert Yen
yonhyaku-en
Visum *biza*
Vitamintabletten

bitamin-jōzai
Volkskunst (j.) *mingei*
volle Pension *geshuku*
voraus *saki*
Vorsicht! *Ki o tsukete!*
Vulkan *kazan*

— W —

Wachholderschnaps
jin
Wagen (Zug) *kyakusha*
W. erster Klasse
ittōsha
W. zweiter Klasse
nitōsha
Wald *mori*
Wandschirm (j.) *byōbu*
Wann? *Itsu?*
Warenhaus *depāto*
warm *atatakai*
Wärmflasche
yutampo
Wartesaal *machiai-*

shitsu
Wartezimmer
machiai-shitsu
Warum? *Dō shite?*
Was? *Nani?*
Waschen-Legen
shampū-setto
Waschlappen (j.)
tenugui
Was geschieht?
Nani ka arimashita ka?
**Was ist der Wechsel-
kurs?** *Kawase-sōba wa
ikura desu ka?*
Was ist dies (das)?

Kore (sore) wa nan desu ka?

Was ist los?
Dō shimashita ka?

Wasser *mizu*
ein Glas W.
mizu ippai
Eisw. *aisu-uōtā*
heisses W. *o-yu*
kaltes W. *tsumetai mizu*
Salzw. *shio-mizu*
Trinkw. *nomi mizu*

Wasserfall *taki*

Wassermelone *suika*

Was wollen Sie?
Nan deshō ka?

Watte *dasshimen*

Wechselkurs *kawase-sōba*
Was ist der W.?
Kawase-sōba wa ikura desu ka?

Weg
Können Sie mir den W. zeigen?
Annai shite kuremasu ka?

weich gekochtes Ei
hanjuku-tamago

Weihrauch *kō*

Weihrauchbehälter
kōro

Wein *budōshu*

Weinbrand *burandē*

Weinkarte *wain-risuto*

weiss *shiro*

weit (fern) *tōi*

Welcher? (zwischen zwei) *Dochira?*

Welcher? (von mehreren) *Dore?*

Wer? *Donata?*

Wer ist da?
Donata desu ka?

Westen *nishi*

Wetter *tenki*

Whisky *uisukī*
doppelter W.
daburu uisukī

Wie? *Dono yōni?*

Wiederholen Sie das bitte. *Mō ichido itte kudasai.*

Wie geht's? *Ikaga desu ka?*

125

Wie sagen Sie das auf japanisch? *Sore wa Nihongo de nan to iimasu ka?*

Wieviel kostet es? *Ikura desu ka?*

Wieviel Uhr ist es? *Nanji desu ka?*

Wind *kaze*

Winter *fuyu*

Winterurlaubsort *sukī-jō*

wissen Ich weiss es nicht. *Shirimasen.*

Wo? *Doko?*

Wodka *uokka*

Wo ist der Fernsprecher? *Denwa wa doko desu ka?*

Wo ist die Toilette? (Damen) *O-tearai wa doko desu ka?*

Wo ist die Toilette? (Herren) *Tearai wa doko desu ka?*

Wo kann ich einen Arzt (Zahnarzt) finden? *Isha (haisha) wa doko desu ka?*

Wo kann ich ein Überseetelegramm (Telegramm) absenden? *Kokusai dempō (dempō) wa doko de utemasu ka?*

wollen Was w. Sie? *Nan deshō ka?*

Wurst *sōsēji*

— Z —

Zahn *ha*
Zahnarzt *haisha*
   Wo kann ich einen Z.
   finden?
   *Haisha wa doko desu
   ka?*
Zahnbürste *ha-burashi*
Zahnfleisch *haguki*
Zahnpaste *ha-migaki*
Zahnstocher *tsumayōji*
Zahnweh *ha no itami*
Zehe *ashi no yubi*
Zehennagel *ashi no
   tsume*
zehn (in Bezug auf
   Dinge) *tō*
zehn (in Bezug auf Per-
   sonen) *jūnin*
zehntausend Yen
   ichiman-en
zehn Yen *jū-en*
Zeitung *shimbun*

Zentimeter *senchi
   mētoru*
Zigarre *hamaki*
   eine Schachtel Z.
   hamaki hitohako
Zigarette *tabako*
   ein Paket Z.
   tabako hitohako
Zimmer *heya*
Zimmermädchen
   jochū
Zimmernummer
   heya-bangō
Zitrone *remon*
Zitronenwasser
   remonēdo
Zoll *zeikan*
Zollbeamter *zeikanri*
zollfrei *menzei*
Zoo *dōbutsu-en*
Zucker *satō*
Zugführer *shashō*

Zum Wohl! *Kampai!*
zwei (in Bezug auf Dinge) *futatsu*
zwei (in Bezug auf Personen) *futari*

zweihundert Yen *nihyaku-en*
Zwergbäume (j.) *bonsai*
Zwiebel *tamanegi*

APPENDICES

APPENDICES

ANHANG

BASIC SENTENCES
FOR EVERYDAY SITUATIONS

PHRASES COURANTES
POUR DES SITUATIONS JOURNALIERES

SÄTZE FÜR ALLTÄGLICHE SITUATIONEN

English	Français
CIVILITIES	**CIVILITES**

Good morning!	Bonjour!
Good afternoon!	Bon après-midi!
Good evening!	Bonsoir!
Hello! *(same as above depending upon time)*	
Good night!	Bonsoir! (tard)
How do you do? I'm happy to meet you.	Enchanté de faire votre connaissance.
How are you?	Comment allez-vous?
Pardon me!	Pardonnez-moi!
I'm sorry! (Excuse me!)	Excusez-moi!
Goodbye!	Au revoir!

WEATHER	**LE TEMPS**
It's cloudy.	Il y a des nuages.
It's cold.	Il fait froid.
It's foggy.	Il fait du brouillard.
It's hot.	Il fait chaud.
It's raining.	Il pleut.
It's snowing.	Il neige.

Deutsch	Nihongo
HÖFLICHKEITEN	AISATSU

Guten Morgen!	O-hayō gozaimasu!
Guten Tag!	Konnichi wa!
Guten Abend!	Komban wa!

Gute Nacht!	O-yasumi nasai!
Es freut mich, Sie kennen zu lernen.	Hajimemashite. Dōzo yoroshiku.
Wie geht's?	Ikaga desu ka?
Verzeihen Sie!	Sumimasen!
Entschuldigen Sie!	Gomen nasai!
Auf Wiedersehen!	Sayonara!

WETTER	TENKI
Es ist wolkig.	Kumotte imasu.
Es ist kalt.	Samui desu.
Es ist neblig.	Kiri ga kakatte imasu.
Es ist heiss.	Atsui desu.
Es regnet.	Ame ga futte imasu.
Es schneit.	Yuki ga futte imasu.

English	Français
WEATHER	LE TEMPS
It's windy.	Il fait du vent.
The sun is shining.	Il fait du soleil.
It's a bad day.	Il fait mauvais.
It's a nice day.	Il fait beau.

PLANE & TRAIN	AVION & TRAIN
How much is one ticket to —?	Combien un billet pour — coûte-il?
I want a round-trip ticket.	Je veux un billet d'aller et retour.
What time does the plane (train) leave?	A quelle heure part l'avion (le train)?
What time does the plane (train) arrive?	A quelle heure arrive l'avion (le train)?
What time will we arrive at —?	A quelle heure arriverons-nous à —?
Is the plane (train) on time?	Est-ce que l'avion (le train) est à l'heure?
From which gate (track) does it leave?	De quelle porte (quel quai) part-il?

Deutsch	Nihongo
WETTER	**TENKI**

Es ist windig.	Kaze no tsuyoi hi desu.
Die Sonne scheint.	Hi ga tette imasu.
Es ist ein schlechter Tag.	Warui tenki desu.
Es ist ein schöner Tag.	Ii tenki desu.

Deutsch	Nihongo
FLUGZEUG & ZUG	**HIKŌKI TO KISHA**

Was kostet eine Fahrkarte nach —?	— made wa ikura desu ka?
Ich möchte eine Rückfahrkarte haben.	Ōfuku-kippu o kudasai.
Um wieviel Uhr fliegt das Flugzeug (fährt der Zug) ab?	Hikōki (kisha) wa nanji ni demasu ka?
Um wieviel Uhr kommt das Flugzeug (der Zug) an?	Hikōki (kisha) wa nanji ni tsukimasu ka?
Um wieviel Uhr kommen wir in — an?	— e nanji ni tsukimasu ka?
Ist das Flugzeug (der Zug) pünktlich?	Hikōki (kisha) wa jikandōri desu ka?
Von welchem Gate (Bahnsteig) geht es ab?	Nanban gēto (sen) kara demasu ka?

English	Français
PLANE & TRAIN	AVION & TRAIN

English	Français
Is this the train to —?	Est-ce le train pour —?
I want an upper (lower) berth.	Je veux une couchette supérieure (inférieure).
Is there a dining car on the train?	Y a-t-il un wagon-restaurant?
Here is my baggage.	Voici mes bagages.
Is this seat empty?	Est-ce que cette place est libre?
This seat is taken.	Cette place est occupée.
I get airsick.	L'avion me rend malade.
I need a porter.	J'ai besoin d'un porteur.

HOTEL	L'HÔTEL
I want a single (double) room with bath.	Je veux une chambre à un (deux) lit(s) avec salle de bain.
I want a single (double) room without bath.	Je veux une chambre à un (deux) lit(s) sans salle de bain.

136

Deutsch	Nihongo
FLUGZEUG & ZUG	HIKŌKI TO KISHA
Ist dies der Zug nach —?	Kono kisha wa — yuki desu ka?
Ich möchte eine obere (untere) Koje haben.	Jōdan betto (gedan betto) o kudasai.
Hat der Zug einen Speisewagen?	Shokudōsha ga arimasu ka?
Hier ist mein Gepäck.	Kore ga watashi no nimotsu desu.
Ist dieser Platz frei?	Kono seki wa aite imasu ka?
Dieser Platz ist besetzt.	Kono seki wa fusagatte imasu.
Ich leide an Luftkrankheit.	Watashi wa hikōki ni yoimasu.
Ich brauche einen Gepäckträger.	Akabō-san wa imasen ka?

HOTEL	HOTERU
Ich möchte ein Einzelzimmer (Doppelzimmer) mit Bad.	Basu-tsuki no shinguru (daburu) rūmu ga arimasu ka?
Ich möchte ein Einzelzimmer (Doppelzimmer) ohne Bad.	Basu ga tsuite inai shinguru (daburu) rūmu ga arimasu ka?

137

English	Français
HOTEL	L'HÔTEL
What are the rates?	C'est combien?
I have a reservation.	J'ai déjà fait réserver.
What time do the shops open?	A quelle heure ouvrent les magasins?
Where is a telephone?	Où se trouve le téléphone?
Where can I send a cable (telegram)?	Où puis-je envoyer un câblogramme (télégramme)?
Where is the men's (ladies') room?	Où se trouvent les toilettes?
Where is the bar?	Où est le bar?
Who's there?	Qui est là?
Come in!	Entrez!
Bring me some ice, please.	Apportez-moi de la glace, s.v.p.
I want this suit (dress) pressed.	Je veux ce complet (cette robe) repassé(e).
Will you have this dress (suit) cleaned?	Voulez-vous faire nettoyer cette robe (ce complet)?
Will you take care of this laundry?	Voulez-vous faire laver ce linge?

Deutsch	Nihongo
HOTEL	HOTERU

Deutsch	Nihongo
Wieviel kostet es?	Ikura desu ka?
Ich habe schon bestellt.	Watashi wa yoyaku o shite imasu.
Um wieviel Uhr öffen die Läden?	Nanji ni mise ga akimasu ka?
Wo ist der Fernsprecher?	Denwa wa doko desu ka?
Wo kann ich ein Überseetelegramm (Telegramm) absenden?	Kokusai dempō (dempō) wa doko de utemasu ka?
Wo ist die Toilette?	Tearai (o-tearai) wa doko desu ka?
Wo ist die Bar?	Bā wa doko desu ka?
Wer ist da?	Donata desu ka?
Herein!	O-hairi kudasai.
Bringen Sie mir bitte etwas Eis.	Kōri o motte kite kudasai.
Ich möchte diesen Anzug (dieses Kleid) gebügelt haben.	Kono sebiro (doresu) ni airon o kakete kudasai.
Würden Sie dieses Kleid (diesen Anzug) reinigen lassen?	Kono doresu (sebiro) o kurīningu ni dashite kudasai.
Würden Sie bitte diese Wäsche waschen lassen?	Kore o sentaku shite kudasai.

English	Français
HOTEL	L'HÔTEL
Will you have the bags taken down?	Voulez-vous faire descendre mes bagages?
May I have my bill, please?	La note, s.v.p.
Are the service charge and tax included?	Est-ce que service et taxe sont compris?
Will you take a traveler's check?	Acceptez-vous un chèque de voyage?

RESTAURANT	LE RESTAURANT
A table for two (three), please.	Une table pour deux (trois), s.v.p.
Waiter! (Waitress!)	Garçon! (Serveuse!)
Bring the menu, please.	Apportez la carte, s.v.p.
Bring the wine list, please.	Apportez la carte des vins, s.v.p.
I'm hungry.	J'ai faim.
I'm thirsty.	J'ai soif.

Deutsch	Nihongo
HOTEL	**HOTERU**

Lassen Sie bitte mein Gepäck herunter- bringen.

Kaban o oroshite kudasai.

Machen Sie bitte meine Rechnung fertig.

Kaikei o shite kudasai.

Sind Bedienung und Steuer einbegriffen?

Sābisu-ryō to zeikin wa haitte imasu ka?

Nehmen Sie einen Reisescheck?

Toraberā chekku de ii desu ka?

RESTAURANT	**RESUTORAN**

Ein Tisch für zwei (drei), bitte.

Futari (sannin) no tēburu o o-negai shimasu.

Herr Ober! (Kellnerin!)

Chotto o-negai shimasu!

Bringen Sie bitte die Speisekarte.

Menyū o motte kite kudasai.

Bringen Sie bitte die Weinkarte.

Wain-risuto o motte kite kudasai.

Ich habe Hunger.

O-naka ga sukimashita.

Ich habe Durst.

Nodo ga kawakimashita.

English	Français
RESTAURANT	**LE RESTAURANT**
Two orders of this and one of that, please.	Deux portions de celui-ci et une portion de celui-là, s.v.p.
Bring me a napkin (some water), please.	Apportez-moi une serviette (de l'eau), s.v.p.
May I have more —, please?	Apportez-moi encore de —, s.v.p.
Where is the men's (ladies') room?	Où se trouvent les toilettes?
Bring me the check, please.	Apportez-moi l'addition, s.v.p.
Separate checks, please.	Additions individuelles, s.v.p.
Are the service charge and tax included?	Est-ce que service et taxe sont compris?

English	Français
SHOPPING	**LES EMPLETTES**
Can you help me, please.	Pourriez-vous m'aider?
May I see that, please?	Pourrais-je voir cela?

142

Deutsch	**Nihongo**
RESTAURANT	RESUTORAN

Von diesem zwei Portionen und von diesem eine Portion, bitte.	Kore o ninin-mae to are o ichinin-mae o-negai shimasu.
Bringen Sie mir bitte eine Serviette (etwas Wasser).	Nafukin (mizu) o motte kite kudasai.
Bringen Sie mir bitte noch etwas —.	— o mō sukoshi o-negai shimasu.
Wo ist die Toilette?	Tearai (o-tearai) wa doko desu ka?
Bringen Sie mir bitte die Rechnung.	Kanjō o motte kite kudasai.
Separatrechnung bitte.	Betsubetsu ni kanjō o shite kudasai.
Sind Bedienung und Steuer einbegriffen?	Sābisu-ryō to zeikin wa haitte imasu ka?

EINKÄUFE	**KAIMONO**
Können Sie mir bitte helfen?	Chotto o-negai shimasu.
Ich möchte das bitte sehen.	Sore o misete kudasai.

English	Français
SHOPPING	LES EMPLETTES
I would like to see a —.	Je voudrais voir un —.
How much is it?	C'est combien?
I would like to see a larger (smaller) one.	Je voudrais voir un plus grand (petit).
What is this called in Japanese?	Comment appelez-vous ceci en japonais?
It's too expensive.	C'est trop cher.
I'll take this one.	Je prendrai celui-ci.
When will it be ready?	Quand sera-t-il prêt?
Will you deliver it?	Pourriez-vous le livrer?
My address is —.	Mon adresse est —.

BEAUTY SHOP	LA BEAUTE
I want a shampoo-set.	Je veux un shampooing et mise en plis.
I want a permanent (wave).	Je veux une permanente.

Deutsch	Nihongo
EINKÄUFE	KAIMONO

Ich möchte einen — sehen.
— ga mitai no desu ga.

Wieviel kostet es?
Ikura desu ka?

Ich möchte einen grösseren (kleineren) sehen.
Motto ōkii (chiisai) no o misete kudasai.

Wie heisst dies auf japanisch?
Nihongo de nan to iimasu ka?

Es ist zu teuer.
Taka-sugimasu.

Ich nehme dieses.
Kore o kudasai.

Wann könnte ich es haben?
Itsu dekiagarimasu ka?

Können Sie es liefern?
Haitatsu shite kudasaimasu ka?

Meine Adresse ist —.
Watashi no jūsho wa — desu.

DAMENFRISEUR	BIYŌIN

Ich möchte mein Haar gewaschen und gelegt haben.
Shampū-setto o shite kudasai.

Ich möchte Dauerwellen haben.
Pāma o kakete kudasai.

English	Français
BEAUTY SHOP	**LA BEAUTE**
I want a manicure.	Je veux une manucure.
I want a haircut.	Je veux une coupe des cheveux.
I want a color rinse.	Je veux un rinçage de couleur.
I want an oil treatment.	Je veux un shampooing à l'huile.
I want a facial.	Je veux un massage facial.

English	Français
BARBERSHOP	**AU COIFFEUR**
I want a haircut.	Je veux une coupe des cheveux.
I want a light trim.	Je veux une coupe légère.
Don't cut it too short, please.	Ne me les coupez pas trop courts, s.v.p.
Cut more off the top (sides), please.	Coupez plus sur le dessus (les côtés), s.v.p.
I want a shave.	Je veux être rasé.

Deutsch	Nihongo
DAMENFRISEUR	BIYŌIN

Ich möchte eine
Maniküre haben.

Manikyua o shite
kudasai.

Ich möchte mir die
Haare schneiden lassen.

Katto o shite kudasai.

Ich möchte eine
Farbspülung haben.

Karā rinsu o shite
kudasai.

Ich möchte eine
Ölwäsche haben.

Oiru shampū o shite
kudasai.

Ich möchte eine Ge-
sichtsmassage haben.

Biganjutsu o shite
kudasai.

HERRENFRISEUR	TOKOYA

Ich möchte mir die Haare
schneiden lassen.

Kami o katte kudasai.

Nur ein wenig ab-
schneiden, bitte.

Nagame ni katte
kudasai.

Schneiden Sie nicht zu
kurz, bitte.

Amari mijikaku shinai
de kudasai.

Schneiden Sie mehr von
oben (von den Seiten)
ab, bitte.

Motto ue (yoko) o
katte kudasai.

Ich möchte mich
rasieren lassen.

Hige o sotte kudasai.

147

English	Français
BARBERSHOP	**AU COIFFEUR**

I want a shampoo.	Je veux un shampooing.
I want a face massage.	Je veux un massage facial.

English	Français
HEALTH	**LA SANTE**

I feel sick.	Je me sens malade.
I feel dizzy.	J'ai le vertige.
I feel faint.	Je me sens faible.
I feel nauseated.	J'ai la nausée.
I have a fever.	Je suis fièvreux.
I have a headache.	J'ai mal à la tête.
I have an earache.	J'ai mal à l'oreille.
I have a nosebleed.	J'ai un saignement du nez.
I have a pain here.	Je souffre ici.
I have a sore throat.	J'ai mal à la gorge.
I have a stomach ache.	J'ai mal à l'estomac.
I have a toothache.	J'ai mal aux dents.

Deutsch	Nihongo
HERRENFRISEUR	**TOKOYA**

Ich möchte mein Haar gewaschen haben. — Atama o aratte kudasai.

Ich möchte eine Gesichtsmassage haben. — Kao no massāji o shite kudasai.

Deutsch	Nihongo
KRANKHEITEN	**KENKO**

Ich fühle mich krank. — Kibun ga waruku narimashita.

Ich fühle mich schwindlig. — Memai ga shimasu.

Ich fühle mich schwach. — Ki ga tōku narisō desu.

Mir ist schlecht. — Hakike ga shimasu.

Ich habe Fieber. — Netsu ga arimasu.

Ich habe Kopfschmerzen. — Atama ga itai desu.

Ich habe Ohrenschmerzen. — Mimi ga itai desu.

Ich habe Nasenbluten. — Hanaji ga demashita.

Ich habe hier Schmerzen. — Koko ga itai desu.

Ich habe Halsschmerzen. — Nodo ga itai desu.

Ich habe Magenschmerzen. — O-naka ga itai desu.

Ich habe Zahnschmerzen. — Ha ga itai desu.

HEALTH — LA SANTE

English	Français
I have indigestion.	Je digère mal.
I've caught a cold.	Je suis enrhumé.
I've cut myself here.	Je me suis coupé ici.
I've lost a filling.	J'ai perdu un plombage.
I've sprained my ankle.	Je me suis foulé la cheville.
Please call a doctor.	Faites venir un médecin, s.v.p.
Where can I find a doctor (dentist)?	Où puis-je trouver un médecin (dentiste)?

Deutsch	Nihongo
KRANKHEITEN	KENKO

Ich habe Magen-verstimmung.
O-naka o kowashi-mashita.

Ich bin erkältet.
Kaze o hikimashita.

Ich habe mich hier geschnitten.
Koko o kitte shimai-mashita.

Ich habe eine Plombe verloren.
Ha no tsumemono ga toremashita.

Ich habe meinen Knöchel verrenkt.
Ashikubi o nenza shimashita.

Rufen Sie bitte einen Arzt.
Isha o yonde kudasai.

Wo kann ich einen Arzt (Zahnarzt) finden?
Isha (haisha) wa doko desu ka?

TABLES · TABLE · TABELLE

MONEY CONVERSION

YEN	US$ (¥260)	CAN$ (¥260)	AUST$ (¥370)
5	0.02	0.02	0.01
10	0.04	0.04	0.03
50	0.19	0.19	0.14
100	0.38	0.38	0.27
200	0.77	0.77	0.54
300	1.15	1.15	0.81
400	1.54	1.54	1.08
500	1.92	1.92	1.35
1,000	3.85	3.85	2.70
5,000	19.23	19.23	13.51
10,000	38.46	38.46	27.03
100,000	384.62	384.62	270.27

COURS DU CHANGE		GELDUMRECHNUNG	
NZ$ (¥350)	£STG (¥640)	FFR (¥55)	DM (¥88)
0.01	0.01	0.09	0.06
0.03	0.02	0.18	0.11
0.14	0.08	0.91	0.57
0.29	0.16	1.82	1.14
0.57	0.31	3.64	2.27
0.86	0.47	5.45	3.41
1.14	0.63	7.27	4.55
1.43	0.78	9.09	5.68
2.86	1.56	18.18	11.36
14.29	7.81	90.91	56.82
28.57	15.63	181.82	113.64
285.71	156.25	1,818.18	1,136.36

153

DISTANCE TABLE TEMPERATURE TABLE

Kilometers		Miles		Centigrade		Fahrenheit
1	=	0.6		−18	=	0
5	=	3		−10	=	14
10	=	6		−5	=	23
20	=	12		0	freezing	32
30	=	19		5	=	41
40	=	25		10	=	50
50	=	31		15	=	59
60	=	37		20	=	68
70	=	44		25	=	77
80	=	50		30	=	86
90	=	56		37	body temp.	98.6
100	=	62		40	=	104
200	=	124		50	=	122
300	=	186		100	boiling	212
400	=	249				
500	=	311				
1,000	=	622				

ELDORA S. THORLIN, at the present living in Japan, grew up in the United States, where she obtained a master's degree in French at Middlebury College in Vermont. After her studies, Mrs. Thorlin embarked on worldwide travel, living in Brazil, China, Austria, and Italy. Her extended stays in these foreign countries made her very much aware of the lack of accurate, up-to-date, colloquial dictionaries. In Japan Mrs. Thorlin helped herself and others by first compiling, together with Noah S. Brannen, *Everyday Japanese* (Tokyo, 1969), and now this quadrilingual word-and-phrase book for tourists.

OTHER TUTTLE BOOKS ON JAPANESE

A Japanese Reader: Graded Lessons in the Modern Language *by Roy Andrew Miller*

Basic Japanese Conversation Dictionary (English-Japanese, Japanese-English) *by Samuel E. Martin*

Let's Study Japanese *by Jun Maeda*

Read Japanese Today *by Len Walsh*

A Guide to Reading and Writing Japanese: The 1,850 Basic Characters and the Kana Syllabaries *edited by Florence Sakade*

Easy Japanese: A Direct Approach to Immediate Conversation *by Samuel E. Martin*

Essential Japanese: An Introduction to the Standard Colloquial Language (3rd revised edition) *by Samuel E. Martin*

The Modern Reader's Japanese-English Character Dictionary: Revised Edition *by Andrew N. Nelson*

CHARLES E. TUTTLE COMPANY:
PUBLISHERS

Rutland, Vermont & Tokyo, Japan